Sunshine Preferred

SUNSHINE PREFERRED

The Philosophy of
An Ordinary Woman

BY

ANNE ELLIS

University of Nebraska Press
Lincoln and London

Ⓤⓜ

Copyright 1934 by Houghton Mifflin Company
All rights reserved
Manufactured in the United States of America

First Bison Book printing: September 1984
Most recent printing indicated by the first digit below:
1   2   3   4   5   6   7   8   9   10

Library of Congress Cataloging in Publication Data
Ellis, Anne, 1875–1938.
  Sunshine preferred.

  Reprint. Originally published: Boston : Houghton,
Mifflin, 1934.
  1. Ellis, Anne, 1875–1938. 2. West (U.S.)—Biography.
I. Title.
CT275.E38515A33 1984   978'.02'0924 [B]   84-5141
ISBN 0-8032-1810-9
ISBN 0-8032-6709-6 (pbk.)

Reprinted by arrangement with Houghton Mifflin Company

TO

MY CHILDREN

Don't read this book unless you are a person who never has been ill, or who is now ill, or who is just recovering from illness, or who hopes never to be ill. Such is the advice of

ANNE ELLIS

SUNSHINE PREFERRED

. .

CHAPTER I

It's what we 'ain't got,' not what we have, that makes us happy.

A. E.

'MY SOUL! I believe it's an intelligence test.'

'Yes,' whispered Neita, 'it does sound like an I.Q.'

'Do you suppose,' I gasped anxiously, 'every patient entering a sanitarium has to pass such a test?'

Without giving her a chance to answer, I went on peevishly:

'I'm telling you right now I positively refuse to take one of the fool things. I've read about them and know I couldn't pass. I just won't, that's ——'

'Hush, don't worry, everything will be all right,' Neita said soothingly. 'Let's listen and perhaps we can learn something.'

So we sat on the narrow bed — Neita calm, quiet, I tense, breathing heavily — listening to

[1]

the perfectly audible voices coming through the thin partition. A man's voice, young, cultured, slow, deeply interested, propounded the questions while the girl's voice flippantly, amusedly answered them; usually correctly, and when she was not sure, so cleverly that she seemed right. She would start with a giggle, run into a gurgle, and end with peals of laughter. So interesting was she that for a time I forgot my illness and worry, and wanted to say, 'Oh, that was good!' or, when she hesitated, 'I know the answer to that one.'

Then a nurse called, 'Nine o'clock — lights out.'

Quiet followed the closing of the door in the next room. Quiet all over the sanitarium. Quiet in our own room. Everything strange and quiet.

Silently we went to bed, I in the narrow hospital bed, Neita in a cot close beside it. There was so much we wanted to say on this last night, realizing that before we saw each other again it would be certainly months, probably years — possibly never. Still we were unable to talk. Our feelings were too deep for words.

I lay there listening, smelling. Strange rooms have distinctive noises and odors. There was the smell of disinfectant, of a newly scrubbed floor, of freshly hung curtains and aired bedding. I heard a rattle and flap of windows, a creak of bed springs. Walls whispered, sighed, even groaned.

At last Neita slept. I could hear her tranquil, rhythmic breathing, and while she slept I, choking down my coughs, went back over time's trail and reviewed what had led up to this night.

CHAPTER II

Some people think they are possessed of ideals when it's only ideas.

A. E.

FOR years I had driven myself, never realizing, because I was so full of life, that I was working beyond my strength. I was a widow and the breadwinner for myself and children, Neita and Earl, and I had bent over a sewing machine or cook stove, never relaxing, not even when I stole time to read or went gaily, hurriedly, to parties, where I sat tense, wishing they would hurry and start, hurry and finish, hurry with refreshments — hurry, hurry.

I had had, too, some political experience — four years as treasurer of Saguache County, Colorado. Years of work, hurry, achievement. Growing years, too, and happy ones, because I love my work, be it sewing, cooking, or tax collecting.

Now one might think I had a fair amount of sense. I thought so myself; but as you will discover, I haven't. I was never strong, and I doubt now if I was ever well; but I was never really sick, and I scorned complainers or people who were always doctoring. In my time I had, without the aid of a doctor, given birth to three children. This is not a boast, but an admission of my own foolishness.

When I started to campaign for my third term as treasurer, I was tired, half sick, and politically disillusioned; but I threw myself heart and soul into the electioneering. It takes more morale than I have to work half-heartedly at any job.

There were long, cold trips over the entire county; stops at towns, ranches, and mines to attend meetings, political dances. Trying to sell oneself to the voting public is a grueling strain. Between trips I would rush home to do my housekeeping, rush to the office to do some of the work which piled up in my absence. I dared not relax, feeling that if I did, it would be 'all day' with me. Weeks of this high pressure brought me up to the night before election, when, after attending a dance, I tried to sleep in a hotel bed the covers of which were literally frozen together from recent snow and rain. This performance left me with a heavy cold,

[5]

but I went on electioneering up to the last minute and won the election. This gave me two years more in office.

After this you might think I would have rested, but I didn't. I'm a fool. The next morning in a snowstorm I pulled out for Denver, where I intended to see an oculist. Instead of getting a good room and resting, I got a cheap one — politicians just after a campaign feel mighty poor — in a neighborhood where there was no rest for anyone.

In spite of my cold I was out on the slushy streets, rushing to an optician, begrudging the time spent in waiting-rooms. I wanted to be window-shopping, seeing the sights, seeing Denver, seeing life. I had no money for real shopping, but I could take in everything, return home and do a lot of bragging.

It was Armistice Day. I stood on a corner to watch the big parade, but the crowds were so dense that it was difficult to see anything. I looked around. Some men and boys were standing high above the crowd in the window of an unfinished building. I decided to join them. They looked rather startled when I, a woman, asked if I could climb up to them, but they answered, 'Surest thing you know, lady, if you think you can stick on.'

They reached down helping hands and swung me up beside them. A cold wind almost whipped us off our feet. A man turned toward me and said mildly, 'This is no place for you with that graveyard cough.'

I myself was beginning to think just that, so the men took time out from watching the parade and kindly swung me down to the street level.

That evening I left for home. On the train were many Saguache teachers, who had been attending the Teachers' Institute in Denver. Late at night we arrived in Salida, where they had left the automobiles in which they would drive the sixty miles to Saguache. I should have gone to a hotel to rest and wait for the train which left next morning, but instead I climbed into one of the already crowded cars. When we left Salida over the snowy roads there were three cars. Six of us were in our car — a Ford with side curtains buttoned on in a vain effort to keep out the cold. Three in the front seat, three in the back, all buried beneath numerous bundles and suitcases. I tried to take up as little room as possible and offered to hold on my lap a huge dishpan piled high with ten-cent-store merchandise. We were cramped and crowded but gay.

We plowed through snowdrifts and came to the foot of Poncha Pass, where in front of us a coupé loaded with three passengers couldn't make the grade and started to back down the hill. Before it reached us, it swerved and went over a ten-foot embankment into the creek below. We untangled ourselves quickly and went to their aid. Fortunately none were badly hurt and they all were loaded into our car.

Two teachers and myself walked to the top of the pass. It was a glorious night, clear and sparkling. The air was so pure and cold that it stung one's lungs. The stars were snappingly brilliant. All around there was a heavy quiet filled with innumerable reverberating sounds.

Over a mile we climbed. My heart was pounding. I gasped as I breathed the cold air through my mouth directly into my lungs. My nose started to bleed. I was glad of it. I wanted to be alone — alone to enjoy this wonderful night. There are times when inane chatter, my own most of all, tries my very

[8]

soul. All at once I knew somehow that this was the last time in my life I was ever to swing freely into a walk. I, who loved walking so well, too — not to mention running, climbing, and dancing. I held snow to my nose and the back of my neck and walked on because I could hear the cars coming and wanted to make the top of the pass before they reached me. I was exalted with the night. I felt the immensity of it all, the sense that I was a part with and of it, that never again in my life could I be small, silly, inadequate.

All of us, with bundles, suitcases, hatboxes, and dishpan, loaded into the car. I wondered if the night had affected the others as it had me. If so we were silent about it, as though ashamed of our feelings, and we were soon talking of bargains in Denver stores, of what was seen and heard at the shows, of food in different restaurants. One teacher, I remember, complained because an instructor at the Institute had admonished them about their personal appearance — their clothes, complexions, and finger nails. The girl who was telling about it thought these had no place among the requirements of a teacher. I thought otherwise and said that I thought a teacher's personal appearance should be considered as much as her book knowledge, and that personally, if I had to choose between a charming teacher and a moral one, I would let morals go by the board. All this from one who twenty minutes before had made such noble resolutions!

I sat tense, with hunched shoulders, drawn-in stomach, and long legs wrapped around and over suitcases. On my lap sat a girl, on her lap the dishpan. Thirty-five miles of this. When we arrived, I could scarcely walk across the yard and up the three steps to my porch. My numbed fingers could not unlock the door. After getting two different neighbors out of bed, I borrowed a pass-key for the kitchen door. And so to bed.

The next morning I didn't feel very well, but at eight o'clock I went to the office where I worked hard on the business which had accumulated in my absence.

My deputy was an efficient worker, but at times there was enough work in that office to keep several deputies on the jump. My house had been neglected during my campaign, and no matter how busy I am or how badly I feel, I cannot rest until my home is clean and orderly. Then, too, I had to make my usual preparations for Christmas, when Earl would come home from college. At night I made candy, fruitcakes and salted nuts — always enough for Neita, too. I prepared also for our Christmas dinner, when I had a family of twelve, but I was not working with my old zest.

One night I sat up late getting my Christmas packages ready for mailing. The next morning I went to work at the usual time, but was unable to hold out until noon. On the road home I passed the place where we were making wreaths of pine and cedar to be used in our community decoration.

A friend saw me and called, 'Aren't you coming to help?'

'I am not,' I answered. 'I'm going home to die.'

It was almost the truth. A part of me did die.

From that moment I grew worse. Before Christmas, Jose and Ben, my sister and brother-in-law, came to nurse me. I spoiled

Christmas for my family, the town, almost the entire county. I never realized how much people were interested in me. The telephone rang continually and there was a constant stream of visitors with offers of help or food. The chickens in town must have suffered. Flowers poured in, lovely flowers, some kinds I had never seen before — a bunch of violets, sheaves of roses. In Saguache cut flowers mean a great deal, as they have to be ordered from either Salida or Denver.

But I was past flowers or help of any kind. By now we had two doctors; one from Salida at seventy-five dollars a visit, and a trained nurse at seven dollars a day. My money flew; money that I had so carefully saved hoping to establish a small business so that I or some of my descendants might reach a place in the sun where, instead of being job-hunters, we could be job-givers and enjoy some of the comforts of life. And, too, some of that money had been saved for school purposes — school for me.

In spite of everything I grew steadily worse until finally I had to go to a hospital. With two men supporting me and another guiding the pen in my trembling fingers, I signed a power of attorney for my deputy.

On New Year's Day, Earl carried me to a car, where, unable to lie down or sit up, I crouched on a seat, supported by the nurse. I raged inwardly to think of myself not able to move under my own power. We, doctors, friends and relatives, filled two cars, which crept at a funeral pace over ice-glazed roads to Salida, where they tested, tortured, and X-rayed me. I think they decided that I was a goner. At least I heard Jose in the hall reproving them because they didn't help me more quickly. Jose, when started, ᴀis no mean reprover. Then I heard her crying softly. Later she came into my room and told me they had sent for Neita. Then I knew.

When the telegram reached her, Neita was in the midst of a New Year's dinner. She got up from the table, leaving her two babies, her husband and her guests, and started for Salida, where she walked into my room, cool and collected. Although I was too ill to speak, I was still conscious enough to be annoyed at a rip in her blouse, which my almost pain-blinded eyes had taken in at the first glance. Reactions are queer even in the face of death.

I don't know what took place. I've never been interested in illness, and as I neither enjoy nor discuss poor health, I've never known what really happened. The doctors, I think, diagnosed my trouble as an abscessed lung, but thought I had not enough vitality to undergo an operation. It is too bad that there isn't some way to measure vitality and endurance. They left us with the dark shadow that there might be complications of tuberculosis — a word which at that time I could not and never had had occasion to pronounce. I had never known anyone with T.B. and it was only mentioned as sort of a weakness, a disgrace that came from high, loose living. Looking back it's hard to believe that one could be so ignorant. I read a great deal, too, but if in my reading I came to anything about tuberculosis, I hastened over it.

I hated to think that R. L. S. had suffered from it. It hurt me, somehow, as much as I loved him. When I read 'Camille' I wished that her illness had been anything but what it was.

I don't know the anguish of spirit, the fear, the despair that comes to a patient or his family when a doctor pronounces these words, 'You have tuberculosis.' But I do know what it is to have them say they think you might have it, and the feeling is something dreadful.

Anyway, the doctors hadn't much hope for me, especially in that altitude. Neita asked if there might be a chance in a warmer climate, but they doubted if I could stand the trip.

We started, Neita and I, without preparation of any kind — not even a change of clothes. At Pueblo porters carried me into the waiting-room, where I lay on a cot until I was carried into a Pullman bound for New Mexico.

I only remember it all as an anguished time punctuated by having a patient porter opening and closing the window. Then an absurd thing happened, which almost finished me. We stopped for breakfast. Neita went into the Harvey House, and it seemed to me that she stayed for hours. I was tortured. I knew that I should die. I knew the train would pull out and leave her. I knew something terrible had happened. Then she came, with a waiter in tow, carrying a large tray loaded with a com-

[15]

plete breakfast service. With a flourish he deposited it in the berth, whipped off the cover and left. With a flourish Neita poured coffee, buttered toast, and urged me to eat.

I gave the tray one disgusted glance and said, 'I bet that lay-out has set me back over a dollar.'

'Yes,' Neita answered, 'six of them, to be exact.'

Then, out of consideration for my heart, she continued, 'The food was one dollar, and five for the dishes.'

'Dishes?' I coughed.

'Yes, a deposit. I am to leave them at Las Vegas where we stop for dinner.'

It was the last straw. 'You needn't tell me Fred Harvey is doing that kind of business,' I gasped. 'We shall never see that five dollars again. All those dishes left on our hands, too. We shall arrive at wherever we're going, one tray of dishes as our sole baggage.' I ended with tears, 'I don't like the design, anyway.' And fell over in a stupor, only broken by paroxysms of coughing, until we drew into Las Vegas, where Neita left the tray and received the five-dollar deposit.

How queer the human mind! Here I knew that any breath might be my last. There were many things I wished to tell Neita, instructions, admonitions, but could not summon the strength except to rave over the matter of mere money. I care so little about money, too.

As we neared Albuquerque, Neita wired for an ambulance to meet us. I was taken off on a stretcher, and since they would not have me in a hotel, a brakeman, who was also a Mason looking out for a brother Mason's family, was kind enough to let us have his room, smuggling us in past his landlady.

Why didn't we go to a sanitarium? Oh, I don't know, except that we didn't know about them. The average person doesn't, or didn't ten years ago.

Early in the morning we were discovered by the landlady. We could not hide with my rasping cough, my labored breathing. She was very kind, but explained to us that it was against the law for a hotel or lodging-house to take in anyone suffering with T.B. We told her that we weren't sure I had it, but she was sure. Otherwise what was I doing in Albuquerque, where each train brought in its quota of tubercular people?

Neita, every whip-stitch, was pouring egg-nogs into me. They sickened me, but I downed the concoctions because we had always believed that they were a sure cure for any lung trouble.

This morning she made me an extra large one, and then left to search for a furnished house. It was a terrible day for both of us. I lay there helpless, expecting, almost hoping, to die. She, with limited money, was house-hunting in a strange city, fearing when she returned to find me dead. Yes, I know that today we, too, would handle the situation differently, but at that time we were doing the best we could.

By four o'clock Neita had rented a furnished four-room house; had had the lights and water turned on; had bought coal, wood, bedding and groceries; had a fire going, supper ready and me moved in.

Neita's ways are so unhurried and unworried. What a relief from weeks of turmoil, from people, from responsibility!

Neita worked with and over me, but she

couldn't persuade me to stay in bed. Each morning, with her help, I got up, dressed, and made myself sit in a chair. I had an idea that when one lies in bed one loses strength. I had no strength that I could afford to lose, as I thought that in a few weeks I must be back on the job.

My voice was gone. My food had to be cut for me, almost fed to me, but still like a fool I sat as upright as possible in that chair. At once we called a doctor, who was considered one of the best in the city. He started his examination, which to us was new and strange. He had me sit on a chair in front of him and strip my poor, thin body to the waist. While he tapped, plunked, and listened, I, at his command, ah-ahed, coughed and whispered, 'Ninety-nine, ninety-nine,' and wondered if he was ticking off the amount of my bill.

When I could I told him that there really was nothing the matter with me; that I might consider laying off for one month, two at the most; that my job demanded me; that I held a very responsible position; in short, that without me Saguache County could hardly carry on.

He never cracked a smile nor turned a hair, but only asked, 'Do you feel able to work now?'

'Sure,' I told him, 'if you will only let me stop coughing long enough to get a few nights' rest.'

Before this Neita had said nothing, but now she said coolly,

'Doctor, don't believe one word that woman tells you.' (Think of calling me 'that woman!') 'She has the strongest will-power ever known; otherwise she would have died long ago.'

'Will-power!' I choked. 'Now wouldn't that jar you?' — when I wish to annoy Neita I always use out-of-date slang — 'As though will-power had anything to do with it!'

The doctor drew some marks on a chart.

'I will send up something for your cough, and also some pills,' he said. 'Eat plenty of good nourishing food and get out in the sun as much as possible. When you are strong enough we will have an X-ray. Call me at any time.'

He showed Neita how to take my pulse and temperature. Neither of us had known how, and today I still don't. Then he hurried away, leaving us unaided and with no definite instructions. I wonder if doctors realize how dependent the ordinary person is on them, how ignorant we really are. What he should have told us — and seen that it was done — was this:

'You are a very sick woman. Go to bed and stay there, in a warm, well-aired room. Keep the temperature as even as possible. Rest, relax, get into a padded jacket, and every night soak that throat and chest in hot camphorated oil. Eat all the vegetables and fruit you want, but very little else.'

But when you are paying for advice, naturally you follow it. So I had the nourishing food — eggs, milk, cream, thick steaks, potatoes, gravy, desserts — and each meal choked it down, when the only thing in the world I wanted was oranges. Each night I slept in a bitter cold room with windows wide open and wind blowing in on my sweating, tortured, humped-up body. Each day I dressed and sat all day in a chair either in the house or on the porch. The cough medicine did not help. The iron pills I refused to take, I rebel at any kind of medicine, so Neita took them and they helped her immensely.

We were learning, however, from the groceryman, the vegetable peddler, our landlady, and everyone with whom we came in contact, because almost every person in Albuquerque comes there in the first place for his own health or that of some member of his family. This naturally makes them kind, understanding, and unusually helpful.

Our landlady had brought her son, very ill with T.B. from the East. In eight months' time he was well and able to work, and today is one of Albuquerque's leading dentists. She told us that she often said to her husband, who was a doctor,

'Do you instruct your patients carefully about the ordinary, simple details of sanitation, elimination, food and clothes?'

He answered, 'It isn't necessary. Any individual knows that much.'

'But they don't,' she retorted. 'Along some lines you cannot overestimate the ignorance of people.'

She was right.

CHAPTER III

God, pity all the worried folk,
With griefs they do not tell,
Women waking in the night
And men dissembling well.
God, pity all the brave who go, —
The common road, and wear
No ribboned medal on their breast
No laurel in their hair.

(Author unknown)

EACH day I was put out in the cold, where I
sat, a huddled-up bundle, whose only sign
of life was a constant nerve- and body-rack-
ing cough. At every house in my line of
vision, either on porches or in yards, were
other sick people. Directly opposite I saw
on a porch a young girl whose mother countless times during the day bent tenderly over
her. In the next house lived a man, his wife,
and little boy. The wife was very ill and the
husband did all the work. Not much money
there — I could tell by the house, their
clothes, and the packages of food which the
husband purchased at the corner grocery.
Next to that was a porch, where a young
mother lay ill. I could see a nurse hold her

[23]

baby up so that she could see but not touch it. Between two houses I could see a tent in which lived a husband and wife. He was ill. She washed for their living. All day, on an ordinary kitchen chair, he sat outdoors. She would often stop from her work to visit with him or to draw a blanket up over his knees, or bring him water, food, or a book.

The most interesting of all was at the corner house — a young girl who, covered to the eyes with a down robe, spent the entire day on a chaise-longue, which sat in the dust and sand very near the road. A young man who looked rich and well-bred sat beside her throughout the day, holding her hand. At times he would bend over and kiss it.

Also in my range of vision were three large sanitariums. Beyond them I could see the city proper, divided from 'Old Town' by a looped silver ribbon, the Rio Grande River.

One day we had a visitor, a woman sent by a local bank to call on new arrivals. She was charming, intelligent, and very helpful. She gave us courage and allayed our fears; told us the best places to trade, and, incidentally, took my banking account. We asked her to send us a hired girl — Neita, of course, said 'maid.' This was the first and last time that I was ever confronted with the servant problem. We wanted an Indian, but a colored girl came. She thought herself very superior, and was neither interesting nor entertaining, which was disappointing since to me hired girls were a novelty. Neita asked her to wash the windows, but she couldn't do it. It made her dizzy to stand on a chair. Neita asked her to mop the floor, but this, it seemed, did something to her legs. It gave her the backache to wash clothes. In short, it developed that she was a stranger in Albuquerque, neither liking the people nor their ways, and only working because she was lonely. One forenoon was all that I felt we could devote to cheering her up. Neita did all the work, and just as she finished we had a sand storm. You might compare various things to a New Mexico sand storm, but there is nothing you can compare one of these storms to. They are in a class by themselves.

The wind loosened our stovepipe which, with its numerous joints and elbows, resembled a colicky boa constrictor. When

Neita was building the fire the whole works came unjointed and down. Flames almost reached the ceiling, and smoke, soot, and ashes poured out into the room. From my bedroom I heard the crash and screamed to Neita to rush into the street and yell, 'Fire!' But no response came from her. My door was softly closed, and alone she somehow fitted together the devilish elbows of that pipe, and after she had swept and scrubbed, we resumed business. But you should have seen Neita. Talk about a chimney sweep! She has golden hair — but that day!

Sometimes Neita would go to town and when she returned she entertained me with the sights she had seen. Mexicans, Indians, and whites. Sick people comprise all but two per cent of the population of Albuquerque. She told me of them, and of street cars efficiently run by hard-boiled motor-women dressed in high boots, short khaki dresses, and visored caps. She told that often when waiting for a car she would be invited by passing motorists to ride. At first this worried me, but then I learned that because of Albuquerque's many sick people, it is customary, and never yet have I heard of anyone wanting or having to 'walk back home.'

She told of the many sanitariums she passed, and of the patients, doctors, and nurses she saw about the grounds; and of streets and stores crowded with colorful people, mostly Mexicans, whose ancestors had lived here ever since Spain had granted this land to the Duke of Albuquerque.

She saw Mexican mothers, black-shawled, sad-eyed, quiet; and younger women, bright-eyed, laughingly talkative, stylishly, cheaply dressed. She saw old men, wrinkle-faced, gnarled-fisted, and youths, ready-eyed, swaggering.

Often she would see a Mexican wedding party — the bride decked out in white dress, veil, and carrying flowers — holding a reception on the street.

She would see long lines of Mexicans with their ratty ponies and ramshackly wagons loaded with sweet-smelling piñon and cedar wood; and Mexicans and Indians grouped around the bead counters in the ten-cent stores; and Indian boys and girls, dressed in uniform, in from the near-by Government

school, or college students from the State
university; cowboys from dude ranches, and
tourists from everywhere.

On every side she saw cool-eyed Sisters of
Mercy going calmly, efficiently about their
business; and everywhere health-seekers going
cheerfully, hopefully about theirs. Everyone
— except the Sisters of Mercy — men and
women, young and old, rich and poor, Mexicans, Indians, whites — all wore turquoise-
encrusted silver jewelry.

She always stopped at the railroad station
where Fred Harvey's Alvarado Hotel and
marvelous store are under the same roof —
a store so crowded with richness and beauty
that it fills one with longing. There in sight
was seemingly priceless jewelry, rugs and
blankets. They were not so, however, but
tucked away in vaults were blankets that
were really priceless.

In one corner an Indian made jewelry,
pounding out bars of silver, and filing and
polishing blobs of turquoise. Sitting on the
floor an Indian woman twisted a ball of yarn
in and out, weaving a rug in an intricate
design, her only pattern one she carried in

her head. Near-by, also on the floor, sat another woman, and beside her a bunch of raw wool which she carded, a handful at a time. She rolled this between her palms. In her hand was a spindle which she kept whirling, in an endless motion, and, seemingly without effort, she deftly carded, rolled, spun and wound the raw wool into yarn.

Outside on the walks, where their pottery was displayed enticingly, Neita saw many more Indians who hoped to make sales to passengers whose trains waited in Albuquerque for forty minutes.

When I was sixteen I had gone through Albuquerque. On my return home I told of a tall, slender Indian maiden, dressed in a very low-necked sleeveless garment made of soft white buckskins, who held aloft to the car windows a basket of fruit with grapes hanging over the edge in tempting bunches. Now, I wonder if I concocted that story out of whole cloth, or if, at that early date, Fred Harvey did have such an Indian. If he did, he imported her, because Pueblo Indians are not tall and wear no sleeveless garment. The most distinctive feature of their dress is a pair of snow-white leather boots or moccasins reaching to the knee. Navajo women and their tiny daughters wear long, full skirts with tight basques.

Neita told of notables parading during their wait. It might be a movie actor, not averse to publicity, in which case there would be flowers, cameras, reporters, and maybe a brass band. Always there were reporters, whether the notables wanted them or not. Once Schumann-Heink didn't, and in spite of her refusal to open her door or get out of bed a persistent reporter caught a glimpse of her — enough to report in the next day's paper that she wore old-fashioned, high-necked, long-sleeved nightgowns.

Always Neita returned with the encouraging news of someone having regained his health. It might be a clerk in one of the stores, or a librarian, or someone on the street car. She often wondered why the fine type of people she met lived in Albuquerque. This explained it.

One day, when she was complaining to our banker about the sand storms, he said, 'Yes, they are bad. But I much prefer to eat and breathe sand than to lie six feet under it.'

She invariably found people kind and help-ful. Once a handsome, elderly man offered to carry her bundles for her.

'Are you here chasing?' he asked.

She thought she was being — well, what-ever they say nowadays. He explained that he meant to ask if she was in Albuquerque for her health, 'chasing the cure.'

One day while Neita was absent, I had an adventure of my own. On the floor was a small rug, a cheap affair with Oriental designs. As I stared at it, hating it as I hate all ugli-ness, those horrible figures came alive and took the form of monkeys, devils, and cats, all sneering and mocking at me. I realized that this was something that I must fight and brought my eyes to the only weapon I had. This was a common yellow mixing-bowl filled with fresh fruit — apples, oranges, ba-nanas, grapes. It was beautiful and rested both soul and body. I had won. No I hadn't — again my sight shifted to the rug, where crafty eyes leered and noses were thumbed at me, while the figures chased, ran over each other, and looped themselves by their tails into chains. Almost they had me. I was about to gibber, then with an effort my eyes again rested on beauty. This time I had really won. When Neita returned, that rug was banished.

How we did enjoy the New Mexico sunsets and the translucent, rosy, purplish glow on the mountains! I cannot describe it on paper. Maxfield Parrish comes near to it on canvas.

When our things were sent from home, I had Jose include a bag of silk pieces, leftovers from my sewing days. I thought that now, the first time in my life when I had had leisure, I would piece them into a quilt. Each day Neita laid out the bright scraps, but my wrists were so weak that I couldn't force them. Then I tried to read, but I couldn't. Even my letters had to be read to me. Inwardly I raged.

One evening Neita was making biscuit, and regretted not being able to make them as well as I.

'Because,' she said, 'like Lorna Doone you have a light hand with pastry.'

I said that if she would sift the flour and bring everything to me, I believed I could manage. Then the thought which needed no putting into words came to both. Tuberculosis. Supposing I did have it? To think of being a menace to one's own! How it hurt! No one who has never experienced it can know how much it did hurt.

One day, in spite of everything we could do, we thought that I was choking to death. The doctor came, smiled reassuringly and gave me a hypodermic and a pat on the knee. He was quite gay.

'You are all right,' he said, 'Nothing to be alarmed about — just a slight attack of asthma which some day will go as quickly as it came.'

He didn't then or later say what made it come or what would cause it to go. (Thank God I didn't then know what I now do.) So this was asthma — quite a rhythmic name. Never had I known anyone with asthma, and if I'd read of any person having it, it certainly was not the hero or heroine. It was more likely to be an old villain of a lawyer or miser, or a fat, surly landlady who wheezed as she climbed steps, or even an old dog who 'breathed asthmatically.'

Once when I was a little girl in Bonanza, a tall, gray-bearded school-teacher out of a job stayed all night with us, and in the night he made a terrible noise choking and spluttering. We children, of course, thought, 'That old fossil is drunk.' But mamma was burning something on the stove shovel and holding it under his nose while he breathed as deeply as he could and held his long beard away from the live coals. Mamma said he had 'tissik.' This was interesting to us who only knew mountain fever, la grippe, or pneumonia.

I never ceased worrying, first over my office, then over my health; I wasn't improving very fast. I worried, too, because I was keeping Neita away from her children. Jack, her husband, was principal of a consolidated school, and when she left he had taken Marjorie Anne, aged five, to school with him each day. He had made arrangements with a neighboring farmer's wife to take care of two-year-old Jackie. Over the week-end Big Jack brought Jackie home and prepared for the coming week by doing their laundry, cooking, and fixing up their clothes. Through long anguished nights I worried, thinking

[34]

what might happen if one of them should become sick in Neita's absence, and finally we decided that I should go to a sanitarium. The city was full of them; Saint Joseph's, Saint John's, Methodist, Presbyterian, Albuquerque — all large ones, besides numerous smaller places.

I dreaded the thought of being in a T.B. sanitarium, among those very sick, distressed, and depressing specimens of humanity. My only ray of light was the thought that when I was able I could go around and talk to and cheer up the poor devils. In my mind's eye I could see them sitting, drab-colored, hunched, hopeless, and myself, like Pollyanna, just beaming, uplifting, and scattering sunshine!

We asked the doctor, who himself was the head of a large sanitarium, where to go. He asked if I had plenty of money — a question which needed no answer. He then advised us to go to the Methodist, which, he said, gave good service at very reasonable rates.

Neita made arrangements for me to share with another patient a small cottage, divided by a thin partition into two rooms. After supper we moved in, and Neita spent this last night with me. The next morning before daylight she had folded up her cot — she had to before there was room to dress. Then came the moment we both had so dreaded. There was a tightening of hands on each other's arms, a reassuring pat on each other's shoulders, a hurried 'Good-bye — good luck,' and she was gone.

CHAPTER IV

Since I laugh all the day I am called an inspiration to others.
But in the darkness of night, when I cough and hear my
    neighbors coughing
(Even the engines in the railroad yards cough),
I am lonely and afraid and cannot inspire myself.

A. E.

AT DAYLIGHT a Mexican boy came and started a fire in the tiny stove. He never looked at me, although my bed was four feet from where he crouched. When I spoke to him, he apologized for disturbing me so early, explaining that there were many fires to build and only three boys to build them.

When he had gone I raised myself on an elbow to survey my new home. A room perhaps 12 × 12, with my bed and trunk taking up one side. Next to the trunk was a narrow closet, then the now glowing stove. Next to that was a washstand with white enamel pan, pitcher, and slop-jar. Then came the door — usually open, and never locked. A small dresser and stand at the head of my bed completed the furniture, except for one kitchen chair and a rocker which later I decided had probably been used in the Spanish Inquisition.

On all four sides, set near the roof, were windows covered with white scrim curtains. Later I slit these curtains and pulled them to one side. I cling to a peculiar idea that a window is something through which to see the outside world. The sole decorations were a framed copy of rules, which later I covered with a magazine picture (I don't like rules, anyway) and a tiny framed copy of Millet's 'Gleaners.'

Soon the night nurse came with a cheerful 'Good morning' and a pitcher of hot water. She pulled to the bedside a chair on which she placed basin, water, and towel. Then she left. I sat up in bed and had just begun to wash when I was startled by hearing women's voices sing that lovely old hymn,

> 'Teach me faith and duty,
> Wonderful words, beautiful words,
> Wonderful words of life.'

I thought I was out of my head, approaching another shore, when my day nurse, Mrs. Allphin — 'Ma,' as I later learned to call her — came to remove the water. When I asked if I had really heard singing, I was relieved at her reply. 'Yes, honey, we always have morning service before starting our day's work. I love it. It strengthens me for the day.'

Then she ran on to her next patient. Each nurse, I found, had from nine to fifteen patients. Ma was followed by a man who took away the slop-jar.

Olive, whom you are going to meet later, once said, 'If there's any person on earth deserves a halo, it's Pete, if it's nothing more than the lid of a slop-jar.'

Pete once remarked about my complexion. (He would stand, slop-jar in hand, and discuss society, ethics, politics, economics, religion, manners, people.)

I said, 'Yes, I've been using rouge.'

Pete said, 'Might as well, 'tain't fit for nothin' else.'

Then came a white-coated Mexican boy carrying a heavy metal tray. With a cheerful 'Good morning,' accompanied by a large grin, he carefully slid it to the bed beside me, and, after whisking off the metal cover, left on the run. I could hear other screen doors slamming, other boys running, boys' voices

[39]

all good-naturedly chattering and singing in Mexican.

On my tray were a paper napkin, a knife, fork, two spoons, a cup and saucer, and a white-enameled pot of coffee. There were also cream, butter, fruit, bacon, eggs, toast, and hot cereal, all served in heavy white china. Later I learned that one could have all the food one wished and that at meal time there was a nurse whose duty it was to answer bells and refill dishes or change orders.

All of these people, coming and going, went into my neighbor's room, where I would hear animated talk and laughter. Then, after a boy had taken our trays, I heard the strumming of a ukulele and soft singing.

When my nurse returned, I remarked: 'My cottage mate seems happy. There can't be much the matter with her.'

Ma said: 'Why, honey, Olive's been sick for years. She has a bad spine and hip, and just now is suffering because her crutches slipped and she broke her good leg.'

My Lord! I thought, and I, as an indoor sport, expecting to cheer up these people!

'She seems clever, too,' I remarked. 'Last

night I heard her discussing matters with her doctor.'

'Oh, no, that was a patient who lives in the San and attends classes at the university, which is not a block from here. He is studying law and writing a book about something called psychology — I don't know what it means — anyway, he tries it out on Olive.'

Thank goodness, I thought, then that lets me out of an intelligence test! Never having heard the word psychology before, I was unable to enlighten Ma as to its meaning. However, I supposed it had something to do with socialism and, judging from what I'd overheard the evening before, I doubted if the young man would make the grade. He did, though, not only with that book but with others. He also made the cure and is today one of Albuquerque's prominent attorneys and taking a hand in New Mexico's political arena.

After Ma left there followed a succession of people. A maid came to straighten the bed. Beds were only changed and made once a week. In black and white this sounds queer, but in reality it was very satisfactory. Then came a boy with fresh water and another, who was a tray boy minus his coat, to sweep. Then an exceedingly well-groomed, white-coated boy appeared with clean glasses and a slip on which was typed your cottage number and also the menu for the day. On this you could cross out anything not to your fancy and ask for a substitute, or, if you wanted more than one serving, you marked '2' or '3' after the dish named. Milk was served — all you wanted — at every meal.

From nine to ten was rest hour, when even the boys were quiet. I was to find here what it meant really to rest. Before I had been like Selena — 'One who walks always ahead of herself in her haste.' At ten my nurse came with refreshment, milk or chocolate. She was followed by a boy collecting menus and another boy with mail, both waiters in the dining-room and just a trifle more pleasant, better-groomed than the other boys. Then came dinner and, after the collecting of trays and another visit from the nurse, rest hours from one to three. Rest hours, blessed hours, when nurses and boys went off duty, and one was entirely free from all interruptions, free from the labors of striving, free from irritations; and best of all, free from people and telephones. Left alone, one was free to think, relax. It was years, however, before I learned to use this priceless privilege, learned the great lesson of being passive.

At three the nurse came again with refreshments and once more took pulse and temperature. Then the boy with mail, quite the nicest boy. He is much complained of when he has no mail, and looks sorry and smiles; never thanked when he has mail, and looks pleasant and smiles.

I could see patients — some in street clothes, some in bathrobes — walking about the grounds, visiting in groups, or going from cottage to cottage.

The sanitarium covered, I think, more than one block. At the front, set high above the street level in a beautiful lawn, were two buildings of Spanish architecture, one containing patients' rooms, the other an office, sitting-room, dining-room, kitchen, the head nurses' rooms, and the dispensary. Up the hill running to the back of the lot were cottages, four rows of them, some single, some double. The single cottages rented for fifty dollars per month, which included everything except tray service. That was ten dollars per month. There were — and still are — I think, cottages running up to ninety dollars per month, with sleeping-porches and baths.

The Methodist Sanitarium was most efficiently managed, and run with no thought of making money. I believe that there were cottages occupied by patients who paid very little, if anything.

At noon I had watched through the open door patients going to the dining-room. All were well-dressed and none looked or acted ill. All seemed well-bred, and if you hadn't known you might have supposed them to be a group of guests at a better-class hotel. In fact, I've never met a T.B. — I don't like those two initials and never write them without a wince — who was not exceptional. Someone has said that a lazy person never has T.B. I believe it. Almost everyone I know has broken down from overwork. Sanitariums are full of fine young people — many of them college students — and in almost every room or cottage you will find people striving to accomplish something. All read and a great many try to write. The click of typewriters is a familiar noise. A number are, or are trying to be, artists. A great many do lovely needlework.

Personally I know of the Methodist Sanitarium's developing two attorneys, several business men, a well-known artist, half a dozen writers, numerous teachers, and, best of all, many marriages.

But I am getting away from that first day. Soon after supper my nurse, who was making her rounds before going off duty, came and gave me a rub. Later the night nurse called to see if I wanted anything — there was, of course, within reach of every patient's hand a bell which brought a nurse on the run at any time of the day or night. At nine the night nurse again took refreshments to every patient who wished them — hot or cold milk, chocolate, etc. The day had been a succession of boys and nurses.

I was fortunate in drawing Ma, who was an efficient saint. I heard — but not from her — that she had come to the sanitarium with her tubercular son and that she had stayed with him until his death; then she had given up her life to the nursing of other mothers' sons. Her pride and joy was the Pavilion, a row of attached rooms, all opening upon a general sleeping-porch, where only men and boys lived. How Ma loved, nursed, and mothered those males! She has come to my cottage, dropped into a chair and cried as though her heart would break because a boy had just died — a boy who for months she had had to lift, turn, and wait upon as though he were a baby.

I think she used every cent of her money to buy things for her patients. I needed an electric pad, but did not feel able to get one. One day, after a moment's absence, I returned to find a lump in my bed. Ma had bought me a heater made by one of her patients. Another time a man who was leaving wished to sell his typewriter. Ma wanted it for Olive, and she herself gave generously and from her patients collected the balance.

On her days off she would often dress in her best and visit among her patients. She would purloin choice food from the cook or the ice-box and slip it to a patient. Often a huge basket of flowers is sent to the sanitarium by a local undertaker. These are distributed as far as they will go, and as Ma knew that I loved flowers, I always had some. At times I wondered if some other patient's cut flowers might not have been minus a few blossoms — enough, anyway, to fill my vase.

Ma was a homely woman, beautified by the spirit within; a sensitive woman, healing her hurts with service; a religious woman, living her religion every minute of the day; an unhappy woman, grieved and tortured by the sorrows of others, but still cheerfully carrying on.

CHAPTER V

How small of all that human hearts endure,
That part which laws of kings can cause or cure!
Still to ourselves in every place consigned,
Our own felicity we make or find.

DAVID GRAYSON

To ME everything was interesting, especially
the Mexican boys. White boys, I found,
when around sick people were cheap, curious,
boastful, either sullen or too friendly. Mexican
boys give service without being servile. The
Mexican, no matter how lowly, is born with
gracious manners, which we Nordics can
only assume.

I have often wondered if parents who send
young girls and boys to the Southwest — the
largest percentage of patients come from the
East and South — might not worry when they
heard of cottages never locked and of Mexicans and Indians going in and out. I can
assure them that never yet have I heard of
a Mexican or Indian doing or saying anything
wrong. While they are going about their
work they necessarily walk in at many embarrassing moments; but never yet have I

known them to show by the blink of an eye-lash that they have seen anything unusual, although, like the Indians, they take in everything at a glance. I have often, however, heard them insulted by a patient. Once I heard a man, supposedly well-bred, swear terribly at a tray boy and end by calling him a 'dirty greaser.' I was angry, and told the boy so, but he only grinned and said, 'Oh, he sick — I pretend I don't hear him, and I don't.'

In every cottage things that would appeal to any boy — jewelry, fountain pens, pocket knives, money, candy, fruit, etc. — lay about. Many patients led normal lives and went to school, business, or places of amusement. During their absence five or six different boys would be in and out of their cottages, but never did I hear of their stealing anything.

I have heard patients call boys from their duties to mail a letter, to come in and open a window, or even to hand them some object beyond their reach. The service was always cheerfully rendered without thought of re-ward on the part of either patient or boy.

A few of these boys had worked in the

Methodist Sanitarium for years. Some went to school, and one I know graduated from the State University; one has developed into a noted singer. But most of them are just average boys, easily amused, always amusing.

On my dresser was a fancy frame containing a picture of my son. One morning the sweeping boy halted in front of this picture, rested his broom, and asked, 'Zat your boy?'

Earl looks like me, so I complacently said, 'Yes,' and waited.

The boy gravely studied the picture, then straightened and once more wielding his broom remarked,

'It's a good-looking frame.'

One day I was smoking a medicated cigarette. It was at that time unusual for a woman to smoke, so I explained to the boy that the cigarette helped my asthma.

'Oh si,' he drawled. 'Once I know man with asthma.'

'Oh, did you? And what did he do for it?' I asked.

In a faraway voice he answered,

'Oh, that hombre? He die.'

Once a boy who was working and, in spite

[50]

of his thirty dollars a month salary, dreaming and planning, said,

'Costs lots money get married.'

It's customary for a Mexican groom to buy the bride's trousseau, also a trunk to put it in.

'If you want to stay married,' he continued, 'have priest an' the girl with — what you call 'em?' He made a sweeping gesture across his forehead and down his sides, demonstrating a veil. 'Some mens go to Bernilillo, get married for nine dollars, don't last but little while. Cost me hundred twenty dollars — plenty — I stay married.'

I settled down to sanitarium life. No, I didn't settle, I rebelled every step of the way. It was years before I sensed the blessed privilege of being passive. I did, however, let go enough to enjoy, for the first time in my life, the feeling of not being responsible for one turn of life's wheel, not having to think, or plan, or do. I thought then, and still think, what a fine thing it would be if there were sanitariums where people seemingly well — but tired and worn out with the cares of life — could go, and, for a time, rest.

I was now what I should have been from

the first — a bed patient, propped up in bed only long enough to eat my meals. From the boys, the nurses, and from other patients, also from what I could see from my bed through the open door, I was learning about sanitarium life.

I learned that if a patient wanted anything in the food or drug line, he had only to tell his nurse, who would telephone a store, and very soon a smiling Mexican boy would arrive at his cottage, the goods in a bag slung over his back. Every store keeps in readiness one or more of these boys, each with a bicycle. Or if a patient wants something which requires more careful selection, on her afternoon off his nurse will give up her time to getting it. That is, most of my nurses did — of course, there are nurses and nurses.

I learned that the very efficient manager did everything in her power for the pleasure and profit of each patient; that every thirty days she entertained all patients whose birthdays fell in that month at a special dinner, complete as to decorations, flowers, speeches, food — even to birthday cake and candles; that twice a week there was a religious service conducted by the pastors of different churches, and that scarcely a week passed without a lecture or a musical, or entertainment of some sort.

If patients wished to entertain guests in their cottages, boys were sent to set the table and serve the food, all without extra charge.

From 3 P.M. to 9 P.M. patients visited around at the different cottages and played cards, read or had music, or, if able — and a good many were — went to town, where they attended a party or movie or shopped.

I understood that many sanitariums had a doctor in residence, but patients at the Methodist employed any doctor they wished, and seldom was there a time when one or more doctors were not on the grounds.

I learned that patients called on newcomers, welcomed them, and sort of gave them the key to the situation, if not to the city, and I learned about my neighbors from them.

Two cottages from me — cottages were numbered, and we spoke of the inmates as 'number so and so' — there lived a Japanese gentleman who at one time had been a wealthy New York importer. He had been ill a long time and was now in his tiny cottage, making his living knitting or crocheting exquisite sweaters and scarves.

Not far from him, in a larger cottage, lived a husband and wife. They came from an Eastern city where he owned a large furniture store. And here in the sanitarium, ill as he was, he conducted his business, and from catalogues sold furniture all over Albuquerque.

Then there was Mary, not at all pretty, and cranky and fault-finding.

One day she said to me, 'It's a helluva life.'

And I, whistling to keep up my courage, said:

'It may be a helluva life. Still, it's the best one we know, and I'm damned if I'll let it down me. I may tremble at life, I may shake my fist, and thumb my nose at it, still, at the same time, I waft it a kiss.'

I didn't care for her especially, but admired very much her style in dressing, her cleanliness, her accomplishments in fine needlework, and, as her cottage was near mine, we often visited.

This, briefly, is her story — a story that accounts for everything.

Her entrance into the world was made in a

basket left on the step of an orphanage, where she grew up, always with the hope that someone would adopt her. A number of times she had been looked over, but never taken. Each time she would stand before the people whom she hoped might choose her, her heart beating high, and each time, because she wasn't pretty, she would be turned down. Finally, when grown, she left the orphanage to make her living by sewing. Then came her breakdown, and now some charitable organization was helping to pay her expenses.

I sized Mary up and found she had a beautiful neck, also a well-shaped leg and ankle, and, when she would make the effort to drag her mouth up at the corners, a winning smile. I praised her virtues and complimented her on her good points until her dress was lowered as to neck and shortened as to skirt. Soon, with me egging her on, she had her chaise longue placed on the lawn beside that of a young man. And how that girl did perk up! In no time at all he was giving her numerous presents and inviting her to the Alvarado for dinner.

Once Ma, finding me reading 'Margaret

Ogilvy,' Sir James Barrie's story of his mother — I always carry a copy with me — said, 'One of my nicest, sweetest patients is named Ogilvy.'

'All of your patients — to hear you tell it, Ma — are wonderful. How we all fool you! Why, it wouldn't surprise me in the least to hear you tell that your Ogilvy is a relative of Barrie.'

Ma, as she laughingly rushed to another patient called, 'I bet you he is.'

And he was, and sent me a book of poems to prove it. He also sent me an invitation to come and hear his radio. Later I went. The radio was the first I'd seen or heard. It was a tiny box affair, and to listen we clamped things over our ears. Since that was a very unsatisfactory proceeding, we visited. When I went in he was working on a drawing, and everywhere were other finished or unfinished pictures.

It seemed that he had been a hard-working farmer in Minnesota; that he was married, and the father of several children, and never had had time for any of the arts and graces. Following his breakdown, he came to New

Mexico, discouraged, aimless, almost hopeless. Month after month he lay inertly in bed, rebelling at fate, man, and God. One day his doctor, wishing to get him interested in something, suggested that he try to draw, and brought him crayons and paper. Ogilvy started, and at once did surprisingly good work — salable work, for which he found a ready market.

In a cottage near me lived a little Dresden figure of a woman. She was very ill and lonely for her home, husband, and baby. Later I visited her, but found her uncheerable, not desiring friends or company. I went, anyway. I was trying to talk her out of a worn Paisley shawl which she used to wrap her feet in and, for all I know, does yet. Anyway, it's not the beautiful Paisley that right this minute is hanging back of my bed.

One day Ma said:

'Honey, since you haven't T.B., only asthma' — 'only,' a fighting word to asthmatics! — 'I wish you'd go, as soon as you are able, to visit a patient of mine. She's a stranger and I can't fathom her. Maybe you can.'

I went, and found sitting in bed, her hands clasped around her knees, a very pretty girl, her gown and bed-jacket of lovely material and make. She seemed surprised at my visit, and not at all pleased, almost frightened. Before I left she changed. It seems that in her home town people were just as ignorant of tuberculosis as I had been, and from the time her doctor had diagnosed her case as T.B. she had been shunned. People were afraid of her, and she felt like an outcast, a leper. Added to this the doctor would not permit her relatives, not even her fiancé, to enter her room, and when she left they had to make their farewells through an open window.

A great fool, that doctor, but with a grain of sense, otherwise he wouldn't have sent her to Albuquerque, where she steadily improved.

I was improving and learning, too. In this place I learned the meaning of many things: fortitude, patience, unselfishness, joy, sacrifice. I learned that it isn't sporting to whine; that in order to keep up your neighbor's courage as well as your own you must take everything lightly. I know, too, that in the darkness of night you lay aside the garment of well-being and give up to the deepest anguish, smothering sobs under the pillow. The uppermost thought in your mind is that the others must not hear you. There were many stories told of patients, stories revealing every human hope, action, and emotion. I will relate two of them, trusting that if either of the patients read this, they will forgive me.

James, a Southerner, handsome, virile, charming, rather aloof, could have had many callers, but so earnest and determined was he to get well that he would lie there day after day utterly alone, thinking about what, I wondered, but never could find out. He was always pleasantly civil, but wisely kept his own counsel. He had a good deal of trouble with tuberculosis, but he was the picture of health. He had been 'chasing' for years, and finally was so much better that he arranged to go to the university to finish his engineering course. We were all delighted. It's mighty hopeful to other patients when a companion once more takes his place in the world. I watched every preparation, and was as thrilled the morning he started — looking so clean, well-dressed and beaming — as I was four-

teen years before when my own son had swag-
gered off to his first day of school. There was,
too, the same tightness in my throat that
there had been on that long ago morning, the
same eager watching for the return at noon.

The moment James returned he went to
bed. This was natural, but the next morning I
noticed that he did not step as briskly. That
evening he did not water our garden — a
pocket handkerchief space between our cottages, planted with nasturtiums, dahlias,
zinnias, and poppies. We watched these
poppies because they gave unexpected de-
lights in the way of smallness, largeness, the
number of their petals, and their colors, so
daring and different. It's thrilling to see
T.B.'s, mostly men, their pleased, untroubled
faces beaming, bending lovingly over flowers,
considering and comparing size, color, and
texture, and the relative qualities of beauty
on bush, branch, or bouquet. For months
James had nursed every flower in the garden,
watching, scratching around, weeding, water-
ing. I am sure that he knew them individually,
root, leaf, stem, and flower. Now he was
neglecting them.

[60]

Then one morning he didn't go up the hill to the university, but instead went down the hill to town, where he saw his doctor. The examination showed that there was new 'activity.' Again he was put to bed for months, perhaps years.

We were fearfully hushed and sorry, but not one of us said in his hearing, 'Too bad.' Instead we assured him it was only a 'flare-up,' while he, with his eyes drawn and disappointed, assured us that it was 'only a cold, or maybe a touch of hayfever.'

In the daytime when he was alone he whistled defiantly, but in the night, when he thought no one was listening, he gave up to his grief. As I listened I worried, and damned and wondered why things were as they were. But sick, disappointed, hurt as he was, James cheerfully carried on without one complaint.

The best-liked girl in the sanitarium was Helen. She was wholesome, friendly, finelooking, and there was never a day when she wasn't doing a kindness for others. Running errands, listening to their troubles, withholding her own, washing and ironing small pieces for someone, or on her electric plate making jelly, preserves, candy, or popcorn, all of which was distributed. She was an inspiration because right there in the sanitarium she kept the home touch.

Then — how glad we were — in the spring she was to go home, a cure! Best of all, she was to be married to a fiancé who had waited years for her. She was very happy and shared her happiness with us, telling us all her plans and preparations. She made and bought new clothes, and saved every cooking recipe, she read articles on house decoration. There was a hopeful look in her eyes when she saw pictures of babies. There still might be time. I've seen frustrated girls gasp and gurgle at a magazine cover which pictured a baby. I've seen them kiss it.

Helen was all ready to leave. Her trunk was packed and her reservations made when she went to her doctor for a final examination. Then — I don't know how news gets around so soon — every patient, all the nurses, even the tray boys, knew that the doctor had found fluid in her supposedly good lung, and that she would again have to go to bed for an indefinite period. Her cottage door was closed and everything was as silent as though there was death within. We talked in whispers and ached for her. But did she whine, did she complain? She did not. When that cottage door was opened — and God only knows the struggle that was carried on and the anguish that was quelled before it was opened — we saw the same smiling face, the same calm, reconciled spirit. Everything was the same, except that before this there had been a look in her eyes which was now gone.

CHAPTER VI

I do right not so much because of any fear of man's punishment, nor for heavenly hope, but because I believe wrong doing is weakness. I scorn weakness.

A. E.

AT FIRST not one moment would I, nor could I, relax. Before she left, Neita tried to get me to do it, but I didn't know how. She would say, 'Pretend you are molasses.'

But how could I pretend I was anything so slow, sweet, and lifeless as molasses when every impulse, every thought was to return to my work? Day or night I was afraid to relax, fearing that I might slip away. I must fight with every atom of strength. I must not die until my job was finished. (As though one's job is ever finished!)

Ma reasoned with me and prayed over me. A friend sent a book which gave directions for complete relaxation. The patient was to lie flat, thinking he was heavy, while the nurse raised each of the patient's legs and dropped them. Then the arms were to be raised and dropped, then the head. Ma said she'd love to raise and drop my head 'hard.'

[64]

I found that each week every bed patient must have one or more baths. I hate bed baths. I have made excuses, and fought and lied to avoid them. I could cajole most of the nurses, including Ma. In fact, I remember only one — full of virginity and vitamins — who, in spite of warning, lies and protests, bathed and left me clean, chastened, and chilly. The only description of a bed bath I can give is that some are worse than others.

Each nurse had four or five baths to give every morning and must be finished by ten o'clock. On her first morning round she left three large Turkish towels. Soon after breakfast she returned, closed the door, and placed a pan of warm water on a chair near the bed. Oh, I'm not going into details except in the matter of washcloths, often embellished with a metal laundry tag. Then with a cold or dripping washcloth she began the torture. Afterwards a towel was fanned in a lick-and-a-promise manner over the body, leaving the victim limp, covered with gooseflesh, and vowing vengeance. Some people like bed baths.

Albuquerque advertises itself as 'The health

city of the world' and tries to live up to that slogan. It is made up of people who came for their health and who are grateful and proud of the fact that they are cured, and are anxious to help others. One's doctor, nurse, banker, grocer, teacher, and neighbor, each has come to town in the first place because of ill health.

There are any number of fine sanitariums, the patients of which are the well-bred, well-dressed, well-looking people one sees on the streets, in stores, filling the theaters, dining but not dancing in the smart hotels. Every sanitarium has a library and usually a music room. Many have church services at least once a week, conducted by ministers from the different churches. The Civic Council has one or more people who visit patients. All organizations have members whose duty — they always make you think it a pleasure — it is to call.

Holidays are made much of. Individuals or clubs give entertainments, usually musicals. There are picnics and parties given for patients. Once I went on one of these picnics. The undertaker, a handsome, kindly person, was our host. He was a born manager. I don't believe there was ever any hitch at his funerals. On this day, while many of the guests were prowling around quite a distance from the cars, a quick cold rain came up and soaked them before they could gain shelter. No T.B. is or dares to be fleet of foot. Our host was very much disturbed, but I wondered, since he is human, how he could help thinking, 'All the more work for the undertaker.'

The different sanitariums published a paper, the editors of which were, of course, all health-seekers. Yet there was no atmosphere of sick-ness about the paper, and there was such a note of gaiety and well-being in its columns that one might think it written by and for pleasure-seekers. A bluff? I don't think so.

A day came when I was strong enough to go over and see my neighbor, Olive. I had never seen her, but I knew her very well by sound. I knew that she was young, joyful, industrious, gossipy, intelligent, eager for life; that she awoke at dawn; that she either read or worked through rest hours; that up until nine o'clock she sang, visited, or played cards. Patients were not supposed to play cards, but it was all right to play Flinch. So next door,

[67]

with an old Flinch deck, they played — for fun — all kinds of gambling games, including poker. At first, when I was desperately sick and could have dropped asleep after supper, this maddened me.

It was only three or four steps from my door to hers. I knocked on the screen, opened it and said, 'Thought I'd come over and let you see what I look like.'

She giggled and said, 'How gorgeous!'

She sized me up at a glance, as I did her. This is what I saw: a bed beautifully white and smooth — it was never any other way, although made only once a week — and at the foot a bulge, which I learned later was a box to keep the covers off her hip. Then my eyes strayed over the stylish figure — yes, some people can even lie in bed stylishly — until they rested on the shoulders, hair, and eyes of the most vibrant person I've ever met. Olive, with eternal youth and the wisdom of the ages, and the grit of — well, there's no comparison.

Fate had stacked the cards against her from the first in the way of family, fortune, and health. I deduced — Olive was reticent about her own affairs — that in her background the only bright figure was a French grandmother who had taught her the most beautiful needlework which she did, and from whom she inherited her tenacity of purpose, her love of books, and her vivacity.

She had been compelled to go to work when only a child. She was so full of life that I imagine she burned the candle at both ends until her breakdown which came when she was fifteen. From that time on she had lived in sanitariums, and at different times had had many operations in many different clinics. Now a friend who had married well was sending her fifty dollars each month. Olive herself earned the ten dollars for tray service by doing needlework, or typing with the typewriter on a table swung over her bed.

She never complained. At times, when her hip would almost kill her with pain, huge tears would roll out of those eyes — I won't try to describe them — and down her smooth, brown cheeks. Her jaw would set in a hard line, but she would grin and gasp, 'It's a great life, Ellis, a great life.'

She found amusement in the simplest things. At night after the lights were out I would hear her fire roaring and popping and would anxiously call, 'Olive, is your fire all right?'

She would call back: 'Golly, Ellis, you should see it! The stove is red-hot and now it's coloring up the pipe almost to the ceiling. It's gorgeous, simply gorgeous!'

The first thing I do after an illness is to stand on my feet. Then, holding on to walls and furniture, I walk to the foot of my bed. This I cling to and dance — yes, dance. I can dance when I am unable to walk. At first, because I'm too weak to whistle or sing, I just throb a slow waltz and swing my body, followed by my feet, into the rhythm. If this goes well — and it always has — I breathe or gasp against closed lips, 'Oh, this is the day they give babies away with every pound of tea,' and break into a two-step.

The first time Olive heard me she called, 'Ellis, what are you up to now?'

'Nothing,' said I.

'I should worry,' Olive muttered, 'if you fall out of bed and kill yourself.' Then, as a thought struck her, 'It sounded like — Ellis, were you dancing?' Then, excitedly, 'You were — I know you were! Here we are so close I can tell when you change your mind, but can't see you dance. Come on over — do.'

Over I went and with uplifted kimono made her a deep curtsy, then with hands on hips I danced, slowly at first, then faster, showing her some steps that probably her mother or grand-mother had danced. We were both excited and laughing. Finally she said:

'Ellis, I just can't stand it. Hand me my crutches. I'm going to get out of this bed and dance with you.'

She did, keeping beautiful time with crutches. Can't you see us? Olive wished, especially when we cake-walked, that the 'Bible Belt' could see us. This was her name for a particu-larly sanctimonious nurse.

When we were exhausted, which was soon, Olive said, 'Well, Ellis, if we don't get well, we'll sure get Strong.'

This was the name of a local undertaker.

In sanitariums, more than anywhere else, we see and hear love stories. I don't know why, unless it's because we relax, get back to earth, take stock, and realize more fully the fundamentals of life. Not only romantic love — as it happens, I am one who believes that

[71]

romance is very much alive — but love of all kinds.

The love of a Negro washwoman, sweet-faced, musical-voiced, her brown arms so smooth and satiny that one longed to touch them, cheerfully laboring to support a baby and sick husband, and wondering, with milk at seventeen cents a quart, 'what po' folks' were to do.

The love of a young husband, arising early in order to do the housework for his wife, who, month after month, lay in bed 'taking the cure.' Then, after doing his day's work, returning in the evening to prepare their dinner and entertain her with the day's doings.

A man and woman lived in the sanitarium, where, as it happened, both at the same time underwent the same critical T.B. operation. They fell in love with each other, but lacking sufficient money, were unable to marry. She, a widow, was charming, beautiful, a music-teacher, and some years the man's senior. He, a foreigner, finely educated, threatened suicide, but instead married a young girl. But the woman, although urged to marry by a man well-to-do, who had loved her always, remained single and went on to the end alone.

Once, his hands hanging as though tired, an elderly Negro expressman leaned against my door-facing. I asked him if he came West for his health.

'No, lady,' he said, 'ah'm right hearty. Ah'm here thinkin' my wife might be betteh. I owed my wife a lot. I never had no home 'cept what her mother give me. You see, I always thought her mother was my mother, too, 'till one day I was so lovin' with my sister — or I thought she was — when my father — he wasn't, but I thought he was — said, "Why you so lovin'? You-all ain't no kin." Ah was hurt, and sick, an' all broke up over it, an' tied my things in a bundle to leave when my mother — or I thought she was — said — an' her word was gospel — "You an' Piney" — that's my wife — "get married." So we did. She was fifteen, I was seventeen. Now, the worst thing we wanted was a home, an' after while we got one — a pretty good one. We worked — worked hard to pay for it — Piney jest as hard as me. We saved. After while our children come, an' growed up. My wife wasn't strong an' commenced to break, killed herself workin'. Then we come out here. Ah'm lovin' her an' pet her like a baby an'' — he straightened up, squared his shoulders, and his hands looked less tired, 'in a year or two we'll have that home paid for.'

Another husband belonged to one of America's best families. The wife to one of England's best. Both had grown up in luxury. For years they had lived in the Far East, where he was interested in church work. Then, after his breakdown and after his money was gone, his church sent him to one of its sanitariums in the Southwest. The wife, instead of going to her people who would have provided for her, accompanied him and, determined to be near him, downed her pride and applied for work — any kind of work — in another sanitarium. On her afternoons off, and each evening, she almost ran to the sanitarium where her husband lay. There she gaily visited with him and cheered him, and he never knew but what she was living in a hotel, supporting herself by giving music lessons.

A nurse, middle-aged, very large, kind, and efficient, was deeply troubled because the man she loved was in no hurry to get married. She told me that from the first moment she had met him and he had said, 'Good morning, Merry Sunshine,' and his big blue eyes had opened up 'like sparks from heaven,' she had loved him. Two days later she was in her daughter's arms crying out her love for him. The daughter questioned: 'Mother, why do you carry on this way? You never acted like this before.'

'I've never been in love before,' sobbed the mother.

She would say to me: 'Honey, I'm dying for him, every minute, day and night. I see his eyes, hear his voice. Why, he will hold me in his arms for hours, kissing and loving me, then go away, I know, and rush right into the arms of another woman — an indecent cat, who is just as crazy about him, and wants to marry him just as bad as I do.'

Me, trying to be helpful:

'Yes, and I bet that, instead of pretending that you are sorry for her, you run her down to him, making him feel he has to protect her. Men do feel that way.'

'Yes, honey, I have. I'm consumed with jealousy. I say to him, "If you love me, how

[75]

can you carry on with that thing?" How can a man love two women at once?'

Me: 'Heavens, woman, aren't you old enough to know they can?'

She, hurt: 'He lies to me.'

Me: 'You make him lie to you. Don't you know you should never pin a man down? If you do, he's bound to lie.'

She: 'That's what he says. I wish I had met you before.'

Me: 'Is he a good man?' — meaning reliable, honest.

She: 'Good man? God ain't making that kind any more.'

She wished her dead husband, whom she hadn't loved, could be alive and see how this man, whom she did love, was treating her.

'The first thing he'd do,' she said, 'would be to bawl me out for being a damned fool, then he'd lick the life out of Sam. I wish he was alive!'

In an exclusive mountain sanitarium a nurse, middle-aged, well-bred, beautiful, sensible, was 'specialing' a patient very low with T.B. and fell deeply in love with him. He, also middle-aged and a gentleman in every sense of the word, repulsed her advances — yes, she made advances. She told me how she deliberately laid plans to break his resistance, but that he, self-contained, strong-willed, realizing that love was not for him, decided to run away. And when she was off duty he had another nurse pack his things, get him ready, and order a taxi. But, as fate would have it, while he was waiting, sitting in a wheel chair, who should come up the steps but the woman he was running away from. At a glance she took in everything, and, being a person who would never say die, she perched herself on the chair arm, and while she pretended to fasten his overcoat, she brought her face close against his, whispering, 'I'm sorry to see you go, and wish that I were going with you.' His hands, clenched over the chair arms, showed white across the knuckles. His jaw set in a hard line.

Then the tears trickled down her cheek into his hair. Then she, playing her last card, leaned over a bit farther so that her tears dropped over his face. He weakened, and right there in plain view of other patients and nurses, and while the taxi waited, he poured out his love for her. That was all she wanted, and while the taxi waited, they became engaged and made arrangements that, as soon as he was able, they would marry. Then she, realizing that he would improve faster, sent him away from her. And now, each day, crackling in her pocket, was a long, loving letter, and each Sunday he sent her flowers.

CHAPTER VII

The son of my son's son is at the white school.
I would have taught him Navajo Magic:

   ·   ·   ·   ·   ·   ·   ·   ·

All that was and is and will be.
The son of my son's son reads a book.
He counts one and two.

LILLIAN WHITE SPENCER

THE Indians in this part of the country are easy-mannered, self-contained, and colorful — in spite of the cast-off garments in which many of them are clothed! Everywhere you see them on the streets, peddling their picturesque blankets, pottery, and jewelry.

I don't know why, but people call almost every Indian 'John' or 'George,' when really every Pueblo Indian has two names — one Spanish, one Indian, both musical and descriptive. Each Indian also speaks several languages — English, Spanish, Indian. Different tribes have different languages. The Pueblo Indians in each pueblo have a different language and the average Indian is conversant with several if not all of these.

I once foolishly asked an Indian pottery seller, 'Do you savvie Mexican?'

He replied, 'No. Do you?'

It served me right.

Most people are contemptuous of the Indian, and if they pay any attention to him at all they want to convert, educate, reform, or uplift him. Or, on the other hand, there are people who see him as a legendary figure. These wish to make a pet of him.

I like Indians, and of course am not out to educate — except along certain lines — uplift, or reform them. They already have a sweeter, better religion than I. And I would not want them to have any other than their own which has been handed down from time immemorial, and has been found by each generation an adequate religion, working in all ways for good and symbolized by nature, earth, air, and water, sun, moon, and stars, summer and winter, day and night, life and death. The signs of this religion, and therefore the religion itself, are kept before them every moment of their lives: the sky above, the earth beneath, the life all around, the designs woven into blankets, rugs, or dress, or painted on pottery or beaten into jewelry, the tunes which they play or sing, all have symbolic meanings, as has every one of their distinctive ceremonial dances.

When you see an Indian ready for a dance, you can know that his costume is not planned for beauty or artistic effect — though it is always both beautiful and artistic — but that the way his body is washed and oiled, the way his hair is dressed, every dab of paint, every garment, feather, or color worn, even the way knots are tied or sashes folded, means something, and is an expression of prayer or thanksgiving.

Indians, as a whole, are very well-behaved, conforming not only to our laws, but to those of their particular pueblo as well. Each pueblo has its own governor, who in almost every instance rules wisely and well.

I know of one Indian, who, when drinking and gambling outside (that 'outside' isn't necessary, as he most certainly would not be doing either inside) his pueblo, was robbed by Mexicans of his money and of a valuable, elaborate silver-trimmed belt. The money he let go, but when it came to the belt he put up a fight and raised such a rumpus that the police rushed in, arrested him, and took him to jail. He was much worried, but not over his disgrace or the loss of his valuables — the belt, as it happened, belonged to his wife — or of any sentence which the white people might impose upon him. He was worried about the punishment which his own pueblo would mete out to him, a wrongdoer.

Few, if any, white people know the laws, rules, requirements, and regulations of Indian government. But whatever they are, they are very efficacious and we should do well to copy some of them. Also we might copy the Indian's contented family life, his simplicity and dignity of manner, his appreciation of and gratitude for nature.

Family life seems to be of a high order; at any rate, husbands and wives never speak harshly to each other, never look disillusioned or discontented. Children, seemingly without effort on the part of their elders, are the best-behaved I've ever seen.

With all the misplaced and ill treatment the Indian receives at the hands of whites, I have heard him complain of only one thing: the breaking up of his home by taking his children, when quite young, and putting them into

Government schools, where, except for vacations, they remain until educated. They are educated without consideration of their needs or wishes, and, as Mrs. Spencer says, they learn 'to count one and two,' and, instead of the development of their own arts and crafts, they are taught to make meaningless cross-stitch on gingham aprons.

Since the Government is giving (giving is the wrong word; this was part of the bargain when the Government, for value received, took the Indians as wards) providing for this so-called education, it's too bad that each pueblo can't have a school where the children could remain with their parents and all study the things that would best help them to live and develop, such as health, sanitation, agriculture, pottery-making, and weaving. I'm afraid, though, that this can never be brought about while the placing of the schools and the staffing, running, and provisioning of them are luscious political plums garnered by the party and friends of the party in power.

People — I say people instead of Americans, because really the Indians and Mexicans were the first Americans — always try to beat the

[83]

Indians down when trading with them. I don't know why, because, when one considers the time, labor, art, and science involved, the first price asked is little enough, especially when one considers that this trading is the only source of income the Pueblo Indians have. They have no Government dole, only their little farms, and when, in spite of all their rain-making ceremonial singing and dancing, it is a dry year and the melons and corn burn to the blistering ground, why, it's just too bad, that's all.

People generally seem to think that the Indian, because he is so calm and unhurried, is selling pottery just by way of amusement and that, as part of the game, he expects to receive less than he asks.

I once heard a girl, who was well able to pay the original price, laugh delightedly when with clever dickering she beat the Indian down from seven to two dollars. Two dollars, for a necklace which had taken him weeks to make, and which she bragged that in Chicago she could, without half trying, sell for twenty-five! This necklace in design and workmanship was lovely. It was made of tiny pieces of white bone, probably from a sheep, uniformly cut, filed, and polished, all by hand, of course, with a tiny hole through which to string them bored in one end. The pendant, a symbolical Thunder Bird, was also cut from bone. Each piece of the necklace was encrusted with tiny, heavenly blue turquoise, cut and polished by hand — literally hand-polished, because only rubbing between the hands can give that rich, soft, oily finish.

Think of the days of labor, the patience, the skill, the two dollars! And so we crucify our brother.

The pottery is tied in an old blanket or cloth and is carried on the Indian's back for miles over a burning road, while he peddles hopelessly from door to door. One dollar he considers a high price for the largest, finest piece. Lovely pieces he will sell for a quarter, or even a dime. Yet there seems to be an unwritten law against paying the price asked. I know of several people who have made collections of pottery, never paying in money at all, but only in old clothes.

Each pueblo has its distinctive pottery, and you can soon learn to tell at a glance where the Indian and his particular pottery came from.

I don't know how many of these pueblos there are in New Mexico, but then I, more than any other person I've ever met, know the least about the greatest number of things. Each pueblo has its own government, customs, dances, dress, and, in many cases, language. Now I can only recall the names of a few: Isleta, the nearest to Albuquerque, where the pottery is made that is sold on the station platform of that city; Toas, the most artistic; San Ildefonso, home of Marie, Queen of pottery-makers; Santa Clara, where the black pottery is made; Teseque, small and old; Santo Domingo, dying to live; San Felipe, with the two-towered church; Ácoma, built on a high barren rock; Laguna, where, they say, Indians are born on horseback; Zuñi, where in the long-ago-time maidens scattered corn meal, without much success, to stop the invasion of their homes, lives, and religion.

Once for a few hours I had the privilege and pleasure of visiting San Ildefonso, a pueblo with three churches and one toilet. The churches are Catholic, Protestant, and the

Indian kiva. The toilet, little used (so are the churches, for the matter of that), is a mark of distinction and belongs to Marie. Both Marie and her husband — I wouldn't attempt to spell his name, but it is pronounced Hoo-lie-ahn, and in English is Julian — were charming. Both were artists, molding and painting pottery which in form and design is breath-taking.

In those few hours I saw to some extent the toil, patience, and skill that went into even the smallest, misshapen, crudely painted piece.

The first stages of the procedure — the un-interesting digging, pounding, pulverizing preparation of the clay — I did not see. But I did see an earnest, placid-faced woman (not Marie) squatted on the ground, deftly manipulating the damp mud into a graceful vase. With one hand she built and shaped it skill-fully; with the other she smoothed it here, then there, inside and out. Her only tool was a small oval piece of gourd, which seemed al-most animate in its rhythmic action. This gourd had at some time been broken and was neatly sewn together.

In no time at all the pottery is shaped and

set to dry, which, by some miracle, it does without losing its perfect contour, without wilting, melting, shedding handles, or caving in. When it is dry, it is ready to be painted. You must remember that I took in all this in a few hours, and I expect an Indian craftsman or woman — for I believe that most of the pottery is made by women — would laugh at how little I really do know. However, in one room I saw a young mother artistically painting a bowl, and occasionally reaching out to jog a cradle, which was suspended from the ceiling and in which lay her baby, wide-eyed and quiet. I noticed no design drawn on this bowl, but her sure strokes with the brush (made of long slivers of yucca) quickly and effectively formed and filled in lovely symmetrical symbols. I understand that Indians, with the material at hand provided by nature in the way of minerals and vegetation, always make their own paints.

Then I saw the pottery fired, or whatever they call it. The pieces, large and small, were piled on the ground and buried in dried, sifted manure which the women had prepared and tied up in huge cloth bundles. At an opening near the bottom a fire was started, which belched forth black, evil-smelling smoke into our faces. The Indians laughingly wiped tears from their smoke-filled eyes and with their bare hands piled more manure where they thought it would do the most good. When they judged the pottery had burned long enough, it was removed, and after it was polished it was ready for sale. Pottery that had gone in a mud color painted in red came out black; the body shiny, the designs dull; like black satin trimmed with black crêpe. One of our party bought, for seventy-five cents, a large vase rounded at the bottom, blossoming at the top into an elaborate affair with three openings, with a graceful handle below each opening. It was loaded into the car while still nearly hot. I know, because I touched it accidentally.

I have already told how the pottery is tied into a bundle and swung across the shoulder of men, who walk, unless a good-natured motorist invites them to ride, long miles to town. There they try first to sell it to stores, then to the different sanitariums, where at each open door they hold up a bowl and quietly, not coaxingly, inquire, 'Pot-tree? Pot-tree?' With the slightest encouragement they enter, perfectly at ease, and stand expressionless while their wares are criticized and cheapened.

The would-be purchaser bargains in supposedly Indian lingo — I don't know why, because Indians go to Government schools and are exceedingly bright. Maybe it's because they know enough to keep their mouths shut until finally they make a trade. The purchaser gives for a one hundred per cent American article, made by the only one hundred per cent Americans, just a fraction of the real worth.

It seems too bad to beat down and cheapen our brother's spirit, his once but never again proud spirit.

CHAPTER VIII

To mind one's own business is not a virtue. It's wise and very, very selfish.

A. E.

As soon as I was able I started, under Olive's direction, to take sun baths. Ten years ago this treatment was something new, and it seemed strange to strip and lie in the sun.

Many T.B.'s are unable to take sun treatment because it raises their temperature, but fortunately Olive's lungs were all right, and the sun was doing wonders for her hip. She had studied sun treatment, and knew far more about it than many a doctor.

By spring I was able to return home, and one evening Ma escorted me to the train. The largest part of my baggage was a paper shopping-bag filled with plants — bushes of tamarisk which were just putting out feathery purple plumes. Ma had dug this tamarisk for me, because all winter, through my open door, I had watched a hollyhock which had remained green. It was, to me, a sort of symbol, and as long as it lived and flourished, I expected to do the same. Every day I looked at it. One morning it was gone. I, who never rang my bell, now rang it loud and long. Ma came on the run, and other nurses followed, thinking it nothing less than a hemorrhage. I demanded to know what had happened to my hollyhock. The nurses, all except Ma, were disgusted. Ma explained that it had been transplanted out by the sun bath, and promised that she would dig me some tamarisk and Virginia creeper to take home with me.

Before she put me on the train she treated me to dinner at the Alvarado. We were served, among other things, with one half a baked chicken, a good part of which was left. I asked the waiter for oiled paper, and made sandwiches of our remaining bread and the chicken — a procedure which shocked Ma dreadfully.

'But,' I explained to her, 'you paid for it, didn't you? It will be thrown out, won't it? Then we are really doing them a favor.'

Ma said that it might be true, but that she had never seen anybody do it before. Neither had I. But how good that lunch was! It saved me getting off the train. When I am strong enough, however, I love to get off and eat at the Harvey houses. Each time is a high adventure. The artistic, varied surroundings, the efficiency, the good food without the worry of ordering, the intelligent service, the clearly stated price, the knowledge that no one is expected to tip. This matter of tipping has the Indian sign on me. I, to save my face and satisfy the 'tipee,' never know how much to leave. Somewhere I read, 'Ten per cent of one's bill.' But I advise you not to try it, anyway not unless you can stand the withering contempt of a waiter when you are dieting and order only one glass of milk and a salad.

When I arrived at Saguache they had everything but a brass band out to greet me. It was good to be home again. At once I went to work in the office, but I did not try to do my housekeeping or cooking. Each day I would go home at ten o'clock and take my sun bath in a place I had rigged up in the ell of my house.

I tried to be careful — I thought I was careful — but evidently I wasn't, for by fall I was again ill, and my friends were urging me to leave for a vacation. One woman said that she didn't mind me killing myself, but that she didn't want to see me do it. Finally I consented to go to Denver for a few weeks, and wired Neita. She and Jack both met me there and we talked it over. Neita laid down the law: I was to go on to New Mexico, and she wired Ma to have a cottage ready.

Ill, and leaving Saguache again! I resented it, and thought that here was another Christmas when Earl would be at home and I not there to enjoy it. I would not have a chance to beam, bask, and brag, as some mothers do, and as I should like to do. Why was it, I wondered, that I could never have or do things as other people did? But as we went up Raton Pass I decided that I just would not be cheated out of everything. I would have Earl come to see me in the sanitarium at Christmas. I counted and recounted my money, planning how to manage it, decided upon his clothes, my clothes, where he was to stay and what we should do, eat, and say. I can always have a good time dreaming. This particular dream, however, was never to be realized. It was years before Earl ever came to Albuquerque, and then only to attend my funeral. But we are getting ahead of our story.

I was met at the train by Ma, who had everything ready for me in my old cottage. The girl in it had just 'gone home.' I expect that from every cottage, every bed in the sanitarium, countless patients had gone home. This departure happens so often that we become used, although not hardened, to it. We think of it as something expected, inevitable, a release, a rest, a fullfillment, and think no more of using the same room, after it is cleaned and fumigated, than we should of sitting in the same chair that another occupant had just left.

During the summer these cottages had been moved from the front to the extreme back of the lot. Also a general heating plant had been installed, so that every cottage had steam heat and hot and cold water.

Olive was again my neighbor, and Ma said when she heard I was returning she had 'had a conniption fit' — a demonstration that the young people of today, I've heard, call a 'green paint hemorrhage.'

Life at the sanitarium went on much as

before, the same nurses, the same tray boys, many of the same patients; and the same interests and conversations, which someone has said are mainly of 'temps., food, and love.' Patients do talk about and pay too much attention to their own and each others' temperature. Personally, I think no patient should be permitted to own a 'temp. stick.'

I admit, too, that food is discussed too much. But meals, doctors, visits, and the mail are the important events which mark the days, months, and years. Love? Yes, they do talk of love. Thank God that they can. Remember that they are young, and youth in sanitariums is much the same as it is elsewhere — or more so.

Of course I employed a doctor. I don't believe that I shall say much about doctors. I can't really judge them because when I call one I'm too ill to appreciate a bedside manner. What I crave is action. I have heard them go earnestly into the matter of a patient changing from a long-sleeved to a short-sleeved gown, but never yet have I been able to pin one down long enough to discuss and cuss asthma with him, because asthma to a doctor is like a red rag to a bull, except that the doctor doesn't charge at you — he leaves, then charges. I did have one who thought I might have a secret sorrow or a blighted affection or something, and wanted me to confess and get rid of it. Oh, that it had been as easy as that! Another, at whose first diagnosis I had giggled, on second thought said I had a 'constipated mind.' Doctors as individuals I like, and I have found them — when they don't talk shop — the most interesting, entertaining, and best-informed (except for asthma) men I've ever met.

Anyway, there was Mrs. Bankston, the night nurse, to fall back upon. She was the best all-round doctor that I've ever found, always on the job and a tower of strength to her patients. Never yet have I seen her hurried or excited. She always knew what to do and did it efficiently, whether it was administering to a patient who was dying, hemorrhaging, or merely having tantrums or a fit of homesickness. All were effectively and cheerfully treated with the medicine at hand, which was plenty.

Never in my life had I kept a diary. I

never had time. At this period I started one, and the rest of this narrative will be punctuated with excerpts from it.

'January 2. Came to Albuquerque latter part of November. Sick again, or yet. Am starting the New Year much better in health, full of hope, and a stronger faith in humanity, which has been somewhat jarred during five years in politics. Am very thankful for children and friends. Celebrated New Year's Day by a dinner in Olive's room.'

CHAPTER IX

It isn't the first cost that makes a grudge such an expensive luxury. It's the upkeep.

ODESSA DAVENPORT

AGAIN I had supervised sun baths, and again I slowly improved. At this time I read a good deal, also made and finished a silk patchwork quilt. I remember one day holding myself up with one hand while with the other I washed two pair of stockings. Then I straightened up with a sigh.

'There, now, I'm saved twenty cents.'

Olive, the wise one, heard me and piped:

'Yes, Ellis, that's fine. I bet it doesn't cost you more than fifty dollars.'

But it did, besides weeks in bed.

At Christmas I was able to dress and go to a party held in the main building. Before this, from each patient fifteen cents had been collected, and so well spent that it provided a small gift and nuts and candy for every patient. Christmas in a sanitarium is a time of excitement — the mail boy loaded to the eyebrows with packages, florists delivering flowers, a special printed and decorated menu

[99]

slip, whisperings, plannings. Once there was a patient who we knew had no one to send her gifts, so each of us, never mentioning it to any other, rummaged through our things and found something for her. Well — the outcome was very pleasing and somewhat embarrassing. She had five scarves, six bunches of artificial flowers.

Christmas Eve I heard Mexicans singing carols in German up in front of the Pavilion, where several Americans and also an Englishman, an Italian, an Austrian, an Armenian, and a Greek lived. Next day I heard that the Italian, the hardest-boiled of the lot, when listening to the singing had cried so hard and wiped so many tears that the top of his sheet was wet. Among my many gifts were seven packages from my sister-in-law Hallie, each package dated to be opened on a certain day. What fun it was, each night to lay one on the foot of the bed, to wonder all night what was in it, and look forward to opening it at daylight next morning.

There would be long stretches of time when Olive and I would not see each other, but would have animated conversations through

the partition. She read anything and everything, ranging from sex thrillers to the classics,
and enjoyed it all. I was reading 'So Big' by
Edna Ferber, and called to her that I thought
it a fine story.

'Nothing to write home about, Ellis,' she
called back. 'Not up to her McChesney
stories.'

And I retorted: 'Yes it is, Olive. You will
see that it is the best thing she's ever written.
Listen to this now. She's talking about
beauty: "Yes, all the worth-while things in
life, rooms in candlelight, leisure, color, travel,
books, music, pictures, people. All kinds of
people. Work that you love, and growth,
growth and watching people grow. Feeling
very strangely about things and then developing that feeling to make something fine come
of it. That's what I mean by beauty. I want
Dirk to have it."'

When I'd finished, Olive called teasingly, 'I
see nothing in that to get het up over.'

And I called, 'You wouldn't. You've never
had a son.'

From the other room silence, dead, thick
silence. Oh, but I was sorry, because Olive

never had had and probably, never could have a son.

She was so clever, such a thorough reader and such a quick thinker, that I urged her to try to write. It was something she could do in bed, and would have solved her financial problem. One day, after she had told me an incident in her charming, amusing manner, I said:

'Olive, you must write. Now start in at once. You can do it. You should do it. Write of san. life. You can't have spent all these years in sans. without knowing all the ins and outs — such a gossip as you are, too.'

'Ellis,' she laughed, 'you give me an educated pain.'

I never knew just what this was. Somebody was always giving Olive one.

'You are so keen on my writing. Why don't you have a whirl at it yourself?'

I went back into my cottage thinking, 'Oh, if I only could! If I only knew how, only had a better education!' But I knew it was useless for me to think of it. I often rushed in where angels feared to tread, but I realized my limitations.

I began to improve so much that soon I could walk about the grounds. Then one day I ran away. I had read that Douglas Fairbanks, playing in 'Robin Hood,' was coming to Albuquerque, and was determined to see him. During rest hours I dressed, went out the back way, and took a street car to town. This was very foolish. I was so weak that the motor woman helped me on and off. Crossing the streets was a nightmare, but I staggered on and finally arrived at the theater, where I slumped into a seat. The show had just started when I began to cough. Although every crowd in Albuquerque is made up of people who have or have had T.B., in public one hears very little coughing, and as I went from one paroxysm into another I attracted attention. The audience, I think, expected me to have a hemorrhage at any moment. I was spoiling the show for them and I got up and staggered out, sorry and ashamed. I crossed the streets expecting, almost hoping, to be crushed. Somehow I got on a street car. My only desire was to fall into bed. So intent on this purpose was I that before I reached my cottage I unfastened my clothes and let them hang partly off. Blindly I went in my open door and directly to the closet and began to shed clothes, when, on the foot of the bed, my eyes were arrested by a black-and-white check blanket which covered a man! I had strayed into the cottage of my nearest neighbor, a hopelessly ill young man who had lost his voice, and whom I'd never before seen. Both of us were astonished. My knees failed me and, undressed as I was, I sat weakly on the foot of his bed and tried to explain. We both giggled. Then a nurse walked in on us. Talk about circumstantial evidence! She was physically, although not mentally, moral, and I had another explanation, a harder one to make. Finally, against her will, she was convinced, but remarked that one would, think a woman of my years would show better judgment than to run away. As though age had anything to do with one's urge, at times, to run away!

After this, since the ice was so nicely broken, I visited my young neighbor each day. I learned that he had been a lineman on telephone construction, and that one time he had been sent out as 'trouble-shooter' in a dreadful storm to repair lines. Through exposure he had suffered a breakdown. His sister had given him her entire savings, eight hundred dollars, to send him to New Mexico, where they hoped he might make a cure. He had tried hard. He was a good 'chaser,' patient and light-hearted, lying for countless hours on a hard pillow, an affair stuffed with horse-hair upon which the patient lies, and which presses against the infected area, thus collapsing it.

Then one day the People's State Bank in Albuquerque closed. Two others soon followed suit. These were troubled times in the san., but not for Olive and me. I drew on my home bank, and Olive kept her entire fortune — a few pennies and some small pieces of silver — wrapped in a tissue-paper napkin and hidden under her pillow. Many had been hard hit, but none so much as my young friend, who lost everything. But somehow arrangements were made so that he could still stay on. I knew that some of the men patients went each day and shaved him so that he would not have to pay the barber. They also bought him medicine and tobacco, while the women kept him supplied with the hard candy of which he was so fond.

I happened to be downtown the day that the remaining bank, The First National, almost went under. I crowded in among the mob of people drawing their money, a steady, never-ending line of them. As I stood, weak-kneed and trembling, against the wall, I somehow felt ashamed of these people and wished that I could talk to them and give them confidence. A man climbed upon something and did try to reason with them, but I felt that I could do it better — put more human appeal and more vim into it. And while I felt sorry for them, still I would have lashed out at them.

The steady line kept coming anxiously in with pass-books, happily out with cash. Like ants they came, like ants they went; disturbed ants, carrying eggs.

As one woman passed me she was just tamping down handfuls of money into a large suitcase.

'All that would be a fine haul for some thief tonight,' I said, and was glared at for my pains.

Several tried to rush the window. Could it ever hold out until three o'clock? Things were getting tense, when just in time two men in uniforms and with guns arrived by airplane from El Paso. They were carrying sacks of money — or at least they said it was money. For all I know it may have been newspapers, but it saved the day, and many of those sheep-like people who came to draw remained to deposit.

One morning I read in the paper that the League of Women Voters were having a meeting in the Franciscan Hotel. I had been very anxious to see this hotel and thought that now was my chance. I did not then realize that so simple a thing as a notice in the paper was to change the entire course of my life.

'February 26, 1924. I've sat and lain in bed for months. Then the first time I step out I sit three hours, rush home, change dress, rush back and sit for five more hours. Foolish but fine. The occasion, a meeting and banquet at Franciscan. Met a charming woman, a Mrs. Cassidy of Santa Fé, with whom I hope to stay later. One thing she said was, "Impressions without expression are useless."

' ... Tea Pot Dome Scandal filling the papers sort of shatters one's faith.

' ... Cottage scrubbed today and Mrs. Gurrell [the manager] brought bouquet of carnations. I walked through the University grounds, saw robins and picked dandelions. A beautiful yellow butterfly on Olive's screen — I'm going through my usual spring longing for a new hat, and being unable to find one that looks worth the price, will end as I usually do by getting something and making a cheap affair which always looks it. — Fine days — why does one write of weather, as we care very little tomorrow what the weather is today?'

Some years before this an Albuquerque business man, grateful to the Methodist Sanitarium and to the Deaconesses who ran it, gave money to build and furnish a nurses' home, the Ives Memorial, and at this time it was finished. Each nurse had had the privilege of choosing the furniture and decorations for her own room. What a good time they had, most of them elderly, but still like young brides in their eagerness and enthusiasm.

[108]

Each used her own taste in selecting, still with a thought for the general effect, and, so far as I know, they put it over without a single disagreement. Wonderful, I call it.

Ma was all a-twitter. Probably for the first time in her life she was to have a room of her own with every modern convenience. She had Olive making exquisite stand covers and dresser scarves, and I, not to be outdone, made, all by hand and while sitting in bed, a white dress of silk knitted goods to wear to the dedication.

It was a marvelous affair — the dedication, I mean — with music, flowers, speeches, spacious corridors, stairways, and reception rooms full of gay, pleasant people. For those unable to stand, folding chairs were placed at intervals. I was enjoying myself highly, sitting balancing a piece of cake in my lap, a cup of hot tea in my hand, when I was jerked to my feet, and on the end of a white string led along the corridor before the assembled guests. A boy moving chairs had closed a chair on the end of my sash and walked away with the chair under his arm and me in tow!

'March 15. Mary, Olive, and I were invited

for a drive. The man had a Willys Knight car in which there was a cut-glass holder for flowers, filled with red, white, and pink tissue-paper carnations. It sickened me. I do wish I didn't feel so keenly the eternal fitness of things. This was the first time in two years the girls had been out, and such excitement, wondering what to wear, borrowing clothes back and forth! We started each of them with a vanity case. Such a happy, chuckly time. They found everything wonderful and beautiful. To me it was desert, rocky and covered with cactus. They enjoyed moth-eaten Mexican ponies, and a herd of pinto goats were a great adventure.... I've just finished "Simon called Peter." I like where he says, "God is always loving and waiting."... I used to have a great longing, a yearning for I knew not what, but you bet I now know. It's simply to breathe.... I am my own best friend. I don't like friends who whine, complain, gossip, or who are not cheerful. So, wanting a friend I can like and lean upon, I must mend my ways. ... Today the nurse asked me what I thought success meant. This brought to my mind a dream of the night before. Some Power asked me what success was. I answered, "Doing all the good one could for other people." [I must have been trying to impress the Power, because I don't think anything of the kind.] The Power then said, "No — Success is accomplishment."'

CHAPTER X

My road through life is rough at times,
With hills that dip and rise,
But all that helps my character —
It needs the exercise.

REBECCA McCANN

THE latter part of March, I left for home, going by way of Santa Fé. It was an interesting trip. I rode on the seat with a highly entertaining driver, who had lived in the days when in order to be a scholar and gentleman one had only to carry his liquor, lift his hat to the ladies, and quote Shakespeare.

We went by the Government Indian school, through Mexican villages, past Indian pueblos, over La Bajada Hill across the desert, then through piñon-covered parks.

It was evening when we arrived, and Sunmount Sanitarium showed up like a white castle against the Mountain of the Sun. Then we saw the town, all bathed in a rosy sunset glow, etched against the blues and purples of the Sangre de Cristo Range. After we had passed the State Capitol and Governor's Mansion, both of which might have been copied from some old print, we entered the town where iron balconies on old Spanish buildings overhung the narrow street; a street so colorful and different that it might have been painted on a drop curtain in a theater.

The driver made a sharp turn around the Plaza by the ancient Palace of Governors and drove on up Palace Avenue. I reveled in it all: a dream place come true. Then right through the water, he crossed the unbridged Santa Fé River, took another sharp turn up Cañon Road, and we arrived at La Casa Encantada, which was for me really The House of Enchantment.

Now at last I met and lived with people whom before this I had only read of: noted people — artists, writers. The writers were the ones who thrilled me. Books were life to me. I had always lived in, and through them, and to meet a person who lived by writing 'capped the stack.'

I was in this atmosphere three weeks when I, too, up and started to write. Mrs. Cassidy suggested it and urged me to try. I thought it absurd; thought that writers must be talented, must have done and seen things, and must at least have a smattering of education. Anyway, one morning before daylight I started full tilt on a book — my own life, The Life of an Ordinary Woman.

One would think that along here I might have written pages in my diary. I didn't. Only this:

'April 15. One month since last writing and I think the finest month in my life. Santa Fé, where I met the Cassidys, who showed me an open door into a fuller life. I pray I have the understanding to pass in at that door. Is this an enchanted house, and when I am gone will the glimpse of being worth while, the hopes and aspirations I now have, vanish as enchantment does? If only the door could swing open wider and I might pass through, able to come and go as I wished! I don't think it would be good for one to live always in a house of enchantment.'

I left by bus for Las Vegas, where I took the train. Two bright remembrances: a porter who instead of thanking me for a tip said, 'Good luck, Ma'am,' and coffee on a Fred Harvey diner. Why can't other hotels and housewives make it as good?

I stopped in Fort Collins, where Earl was at school, and spent Easter with him. Because I was so much improved in health, it was a happy, hopeful time.

One day I confessed to Earl that I was trying to write. It did not startle him in the least. I believe that if I should announce to him that I intended to run for President he would think it the thing to do, never questioning how I expected to bring it about or handle it when I did. And no matter how important the job, he would urge me, 'Go at it, young lady.'

I remember I was all a-twitter, like a young girl confessing her first love, and to hide my feelings I said to Earl, who was lighting a cigarette: 'Do you know, Earl, a great many of the women I saw in Santa Fé were smoking, and I think I'd like to. Light me one and we'll smoke together, now that I'm where you can take care of me in case it knocks me out.'

For a minute he looked me in the eye, then fumbled with the cigarette package.

'Mama,' he said, 'a number of the college girls smoke, which is perfectly all right with me, but do you know — I guess I'm kind of old-fashioned — I wish you wouldn't.'

This time, when I arrived at home, Saguache did not make any particular fuss over me. To hold the spotlight I should have died or at least recovered. (Some time ago Jackie reported to me that Neita had consulted a fortune-teller in regard to my health. Fortune-tellers and snake doctors are, so far, the only people left unconsulted by me — 'And Mama-Annie, she told mother you wouldn't get well and you wouldn't die.')

Whenever I was able, I worked in the office, and my spare time I put into writing, or trying to write. Diary report:

'June 5. Since coming home have taken life easy and have enjoyed every minute of my writing and feel I will go on just for my own pleasure. Always, when other people enjoyed themselves and I've tried too, I couldn't. I felt the want of something. Now this want is satisfied. It can't be praise I've been longing for, because no one knows of this, and I am sure it does not and may never bring forth any praise. At times it seems to me there is no merit in it at all, at others that there might be something made of it. Have sent a sample to Arthur Brisbane. Wonder what his answer will be? [The nerve. It's to laugh. Trust me to do a thing like that. Anyway, you will have to give me credit for not dealing with middlemen.] Whatever it is, I'm going on just for the pleasure I get from it....

'June 26. Home with a bad attack of asthma. Oh, this asthma! I see why people would rather die than try so hard to live. My efforts returned from A. Brisbane. Just as expected. Still, I hoped for more. He advised me to send my material to publishers, as they were the only ones to judge. [Sound advice, Arthur, which I pass on to other beginning writers. Don't ask relatives, friends, or even other writers. Their opinion, whatever it is, is worthless. The only important 'lowdown' comes from publishers who hold the purse-strings.]

'I have not written in two weeks and have lost the thrill it gave me. Oh, well, anyway, for a short time I was happy. As soon as I am better will try again. It amuses me. Since writing Jackie has had a dreadful accident. [He was run over by a car.] I think this is

[117]

what started me on the down grade. I am so thankful he is no worse. Earl in Oklahoma. [At R.O.T.C. training camp.] I pray he is all right. When a mother is not well she has so many doubts and fears. Popular things I hate: Fancy openwork shoes, music with my meals, the sex theme in literature, cross-word puzzles, and, worst of all, Ma Jong.'

It was months before I wrote again. All summer I was ill. My family gathered about, thinking that this time I would surely cash in. Neita and Jack from Goodrich — poor Jackie with his bandaged, scarred head; Ben and Jose from Bonanza; Ruth from California. But we have such a good time when we are together that I fooled them and got better. Jose, because she knows I like old things, brought me a book of poems by Martin Tupper. It had belonged to a man whom we had known as children, and it had been given to him by his sweetheart on his departure for the Civil War. But the moment I opened that book, what do you think arrested my eye?

'Who hath considered the blessing of his breath until the poison of an asthma hath struck him?' Who hath? I ask you.

In August, I joined Neita in Denver, but first I hid all my writings — where do you suppose? Far back in the victrola, which I set near the door so that in case of fire it would be the first thing to be saved. We had heard of a sanitarium where patients by dieting and fasting were cured of many ailments, including asthma. This place I thought quite expensive, but if one has asthma bad enough, no price is too high for relief. Moreover, we are always hopeful, thinking that each new cure is *the* cure. That's the reason we are so gullible and try all the patent medicines that are advertised. I went to this sanitarium, and handed over a check for two hundred and twenty-five dollars before they would even let me go to bed.

The buildings were beautiful. My room was tasteful and luxurious. The doctors, five of them, as far as I know were good. One question that I noticed they never fail to ask is, whom to notify 'in case.' After my examination, I settled down for a complete fast.

The day after my report had gone into the office, the head of the sanitarium called on me. He was a clever man, well known and high in his profession. While we visited he patted my hand, and finally bent over and kissed me. At the time this was the best and most stimulating medicine that could have been administered. I told him so. I also told him that I bet he looked over each report and that every patient listed as 'widow' or 'spinster' got as first aid a kiss, which was only common-sense and showed he knew humanity.

There was a male nurse who was most interesting. If there was any woman nurse in my room when he came, we saw only a small, nervous, gray-haired, gray-faced man, but when we were alone he was a different being. He mimicked and pantomimed doctors, nurses, maids, and patients. He danced, jigged, and cake-walked. He sang and whistled, all silently. He jokingly made desperate love to me. He wafted kisses, and at my supposed rebuffs — I really only laughed — he would strike a pose and tear his hair, beat his breast and quote poetry. When he was gone, I would lie there, and to keep my mind off food — for just at this time I was being tortured with visions of sardines, dill pickles, and navy-bean soup — I would think up clever things to say to him. On his hours off I could hear him at the piano. I know little about music, but I do know that his playing was by turns stirring, plaintive, throbbing, and quieting. At times it was so dance-compelling that both my mind and body moved with the rhythm.

His story, which I dug out by degrees, may have chiseled those deep lines in his face. His father was a prominent Eastern doctor, and he, the son, also studied to be a doctor. Once when he was in dreadful pain he had taken or was given narcotics, and he became an addict. He wrestled with this habit, but couldn't overcome it, and he went down the line into the depths, until he supported himself by playing the piano in saloons, dives, and honky-tonks. Finally he drifted to Denver, where he found himself penniless, hungry, and, worst of all, without dope. He was desperate. Late one night in one of the parks he lost all control of himself and ran in circles until he fell and groveled on the ground. A doctor found him there and brought him to this san., locked him up, treated him for a time, then put him on a fast and finally cured him. All this I drew from the man, bit by bit.

For thirteen days I fasted. Nothing passed my lips except an occasional drink of water and a thin slice of lemon which the nurse bootlegged for me. I was weak, but never particularly hungry, and suffered no pain after the third day.

On the fourteenth day I was given a shredded wheat biscuit — merely for chewing purposes, not to swallow. Then I was brought something called gruel which was, I think, one teaspoonful of cream of wheat cooked in one quart of water. Anyway, it was good. Ambrosia could have tasted no better. For breakfast I would have two oranges, for lunch a large salad of tomato and lettuce, for supper 'fifty-fifty,' which is a warm drink, half milk, half water, and one toasted shredded wheat.

When I was strong enough I went to the dining-room, where, under supervision, they served wonderful meals. Of course anything to eat was wonderful. I never realized that food could taste so good, and I am convinced that had I remained there I should have been completely cured. As it was, when I returned home after thirty days, minus asthma and also twenty-five pounds, I was feeling fine.

CHAPTER XI

Most pride is egotism; a by product of selfishness.

A. E.

WHEN my six years as treasurer of Saguache County were over, I decided to leave Saguache and live in a warmer climate. Santa Fé was the place decided upon — not because it was much warmer, but because it was Santa Fé. Then, too, I wanted to discuss writing with Mrs. Cassidy, to whom I had already sent five letters, chapters, installments, or something. I didn't know what they were. I didn't even know whether or not they could be called writing.

I had decided, as soon as I was able, to start a tea-room in Santa Fé. I had my eye on a perfect place, part of the old Prince residence on Palace Avenue. On my former visit I had talked to Mrs. Prince and made tentative plans to rent the three rooms opening on an inside patio. I dreamed of this place and was so enthusiastic that in my mind I had decorated and furnished the room and the patio. Even the cooking and serving of food had been planned. I feared, however, that I should not get the place and wanted to clinch the bargain, but Mrs. Cassidy said: 'If it's for you to have it, you will. If not, you won't.'

It wasn't for me to have it.

The Cassidys, I found, on my arrival, were in Texas and had left Mary Borrego in charge. I had my same room and Mary cooked the meals. From my diary:

'November 13, '24. Seven A.M. in front of a huge fire in Cassidy fireplace. A restful time, or should be except for the thought continually nagging, harassing my every waking moment — Where am I going? What am I going to do? Each evening I relax and determine to let the future take care of itself, then in a little while find myself planning, wondering. Each new morning I say, "Today I will only live and not care about tomorrow or next month." Then find myself mentally counting my money, about six hundred dollars, and planning how long it will keep me if I only spend so much per month. Still, in the back of my mind I know everything is going to be all right. Am going to start my writing again. If I only dared hope something would come from this.

'November 14. Walked to town and spent five dollars, so after this must walk in another direction. I am unable to understand myself. Am not interested in anything. Is it because of being so unsettled, or is it the dread of asthma hanging over my head — or, I should say, chest? I do wish I were religious or could even have a love affair. Have always claimed and thought that, when my children were on their own feet, I should have nothing to think about but myself. This is true, but I find that to think only of oneself makes one miserable and is to me not entertaining in the least. If this is freedom and my long-talked-of fling, please excuse me.

'Last night I was worried and dreamed of asking, "What shall I do?"

'Something answered, "Write."

'I asked, "Where shall I go?"

'It answered, "Stay here."

'I asked, "How can I?"

'It answered, "Let your soul rest."

'This surprised me awake, because in any of my talks with myself I never discuss souls.'

This was sound advice, but I, being one of those people who ask for guidance and then ignore it, did not take it. I was not strong enough to keep house and could not afford to pay board longer than one month. Santa Fé was cold, and I began to cough and feared asthma.

I decided to visit my sister Ruth, who lived in California. The very name meant warmth, oranges, ocean, roses. So on January first I left, waving good-bye to mountains covered with snow, thinking that if I never saw another snowflake I should be glad. We rode in snow until well past Albuquerque. At Flagstaff, Arizona, they had to put on snow plows, and I arrived in Portola, California, in a heavy snowstorm which deepened with the days. In a few weeks I was ill and realized that I should have to go lower. How I wished I was back in the Methodist San! I went down to Oroville, where I found warmth, oranges, and roses in abundance. I rented two tiny rooms and settled down to write. I shall leave out the harrowing details of a sick woman without money, hunting rooms in a strange town.

The diary says:

'March 20, '25. Since I last wrote some water

has gone under the bridge — considerable lately, as it has rained steadily for the last three days and I haven't been out of the house. I am better, cough almost gone. Am having a satisfaction and inward glow to think I can still find favor in a man's eyes. A renewal of confidence to a woman of my age. I only wish I had handled the case differently. Now I shall never know whether he was a hero or villain. Oh, well, it doesn't matter. I am utterly alone, but my days never drag. I read, sew, and type on the story which I hope to finish before leaving. At times it sounds pretty good, at others I feel that it is an endless round of the same words put together in a loose and rather cheap manner. While I want it simple — it couldn't be otherwise — I don't want it cheap.

'April 11. The evening before Easter. I've just been around the corner and stolen some roses. Almost well and as happy as I suppose we humans ever are, only it's very lonely. Have been reading Sherwood Anderson's "A Story-Teller's Story," and like it, except am afraid I don't understand Anderson, but then he doesn't seem to understand himself.'

By the first of May, my book was finished, typed, and sent to Mrs. Cassidy, who was going to help find a publisher. Then I grew desperately ill. Three different doctors were called — three because in Oroville I knew slightly three different people, each of whom insisted that I have his favorite physician. Ruth was sent for and took me back with her to Portola, where all summer I lay ill. When my paroxysms got past bearing, we would have a doctor. Between times I was taking patent medicine and every other concoction that I or my friends ever heard of. They didn't have to be friends. I've used remedies given me by total strangers — silly, impossible things. I've taken loads of whiskey-soaked garlic, recommended by a Western Pacific brakeman. For weeks I've drunk carbolic acid and water recommended by a lumberjack. The postmaster in a town several miles away heard of me and suggested an atomizer, which at first I refused to get. I finally did get it, and have received more benefit from it than from any other thing I've found.

Speaking of remedies, Sinclair Lewis writes of a doctor who for asthma used 'foxes' lungs.'

I wish he'd gone more into details. Do you eat, sniff, rub in, inhale, or what?

I lived beside the road in a small shack. From my bed I could, through my open door, see the road and the travelers thereon. Beyond the road, fringed with high pine trees, was the river, then the railroad tracks, and the place where heavy-laden fruit trains, going east, stopped to be iced.

There are sheds on a high platform several hundred feet long. Several minutes before the cars pull in, men slide out on these platforms orderly piles of huge ice cakes, and stand at attention until the train stops, when all is action. Some men run lightly along the tops and open the trapdoors in each car, while others, all working in unison, skim the ice across the platform along the car, into the openings, then tamp them in, slam the doors, and on to the next, in an almost rhythmic dance.

Freight cars that flashed by, flaunting names and numerals of different railroads and hobo messages and symbols, were to me always interesting. I wondered with what each car was loaded, where it was produced and how, and where it was going. Back of it all I saw the workers, their thoughts while working, their hopes and aspirations.

I could never see the flats loaded with mammoth logs in transit from logging camp to lumber mill without wondering about the history, the life that had taken place around each tree. In thought I would follow the lumber to its ultimate end, which I always hoped would be the building of homes. There is something so intimate and animate about lumber.

There were, too, the heavily guarded treasure-trove silk trains speeding eastwards. This silk came from Japan by fast boats to San Francisco or Seattle and had right of way even over the mail trains. I could follow that silk, in my mind, through all its life from worm to wearer.

Often I saw bums steal rides and drop off freights when the engineer blew his whistle for Portola. First, they threw their bedrolls from the moving train. Then they themselves jumped, sometimes landing on their feet, but more often on their hands and knees, rolling over and over. Each day, never giving me a glance, they passed my open door. Once two went along arm in arm, gaily chattering. One was blind and carried all their belongings; the other, the pathfinder, had but one leg and went on crutches. Once a gray shaggy-bearded one lifted the mosquito netting hanging over my door, looked in, saw me in bed, quickly tipped his hat, excused himself, and started away. I called him to come on in. It turned out that he wanted salt. Several hoboes cooking a Mulligan stew found they had no salt and sent him out scouting. I told him where to find it in my cupboard. He did. Then he noticed, hanging near my bed, where I could feast my eyes on it, a lovely Paisley shawl. Earl, who had left school and was working for the stupendous sum of eighty dollars a month, knew how I had always longed for a Paisley and had used his scant earnings to get one for me. The bum spoke of its beauty and said it reminded him of one that his grandmother wore to church. Then he asked me why I was in bed, and when I told him, he sat down leisurely and began to expound asthma cures: red pepper swallowed often in copious doses; twenty nutmegs strung together and worn around the neck. Desert sand, taken a spoonful at a time, also sounded alluring, but not so much as this: retire to the top of a high mountain, and live there eating nothing but meat. But the mention of meat reminded him of Mulligan and he hastily left.

Between the railroad tracks and my shack was Feather River; also the main highway along which, day and night, moved a steady stream of humanity: loggers going to lumber camps, miners to Walker Mine, Italians with truckloads of juice-dripping grapes, tourists, farmers, bootleggers — all on the road to Reno, forty miles away.

That was a hard summer. Except for my sister who brought my meals, I saw very few people. I was too ill to read or write. I had heard nothing from my first effort and had decided that writing was beyond me. One day, however, when the hot sun beat down on the shack and I was frantic, fighting for breath and too weak to get out of bed for paper, I had the urge to write. On the back of an old envelope I wrote the most descriptive, most peaceful paragraph that appears in 'Plain Anne Ellis.'

From the diary:

'August, 1925. Again the enemy downs me. Five weeks in the "land of counterpane." Am trying to revive an interest in the writing, but, after straining each nerve and muscle of head, heart, and mind just to get one's breath, there seems to be nothing left to work with. Every organ is congested, every nerve and muscle is tied in bow knots. I think even bones and marrow are in a general upheaval, trying to come forth to the light of day through lungs and bronchial tubes. Life's only essential is to breathe. Love, religion, ambition, family, and the structure of the universe might fall away, only let us breathe, or not.

'August 29. Today I am very sick. Yes, worse than usual, as my courage and hope are oozing away. The tar paper on the roof seems to draw the heat until even the top of my head burns. The evolution trial is over in Tennessee, a lot of piffle, and now William Jennings Bryan is dead and has solved the mystery — and I'll bet he has found that all his and Darrow's talk was as fleas chirruping at the sun — if fleas do chirrup.

'September 19, '25. Tomorrow this Wandering Jew of an Anne Ellis takes to the road again. Don't know just where I shall be or how long. This I do know — that I have but two hundred to do me through the winter. Here I will confide that I think my book is pretty good and believe that sometime it will go over. Kismet be good.'

That fall my sister moved to Berkeley. I went with her. It was my fourth trip through marvelous Feather River Cañon, and not once had I been able to enjoy it.

However, I got better. I always have, and in a few weeks I was able to take a street car to Oakland, then across the bay to San Francisco, then out to the ocean. All of my life I'd wanted to see the ocean. Now I had to be almost lifted up and down steps, everywhere. It was maddening when I'd always been so active. Things were disappointing, too. In imagination my first sight of the ocean was to give me the same exaltation as standing on a high mountain-top, the same largeness of spirit, the same oneness with nature. Instead I was hurt, disappointed by the people, by shooting galleries, hot-dog stands. I was hurt at the cheapness of it all. Many things in life, I find, are more satisfying to read of than to experience.

The taste of it was bitter in my mouth, but in a few days I was eager to go again. I want so to do and see things, to go to places and be something, in short, to live. I will save money, and then, when there's something I want to see, spend it like a prince — or, my relatives say, like a drunken sailor.

My sister was having economic troubles — we always are — and I decided to spend the winter in Colorado with Neita. Before leaving, we went to a football game. As I had never seen a big one, I insisted that Ruth and Inez go with me to this one. They would rather have gone to a picture show, but I, like many others, do things for my own pleasure and not for that of my guests. I wanted to see all the buildings, especially the Greek Theater. There is something about a college that moves me greatly. The grounds, the buildings, youth, to me are symbolical and embody all things hoped for. I insisted upon seeing it all, so poor, patient Ruth helped me around. I loved the game, the crowds, the enthusiasm, the music, everything. When we came out, I fell in with the winners and almost danced with them.

'October 11. Letter from Mrs. A. She has shown the sketch I sent her to Edwin Balmer. He gave her no encouragement. Said the public did not want this kind of stuff and to write about the most exciting time in my life. That's just it. In the "Life of an Ordinary Woman," who is plodding along doing the best she can to make a living, there are so few exciting times. I suppose Edwin wants blood and thunder. He'll not get it, not from me he won't. And I think, if I can live long enough and try hard enough, I may find someone who is interested in the life of such as me, even though it hasn't been exciting.

'October 23. Packing for another move in my moving career. Going blindly following the line of least resistance, hoping for the best, prepared to stand the worst. But how I dread that Colorado cold! Wonder will I ever come to California again. Wonder what the future holds and still I wonder.'

Today, years later, this is being written in California.

CHAPTER XII

The sun drops red through a curtain of dust.
White scars seam the alkali plain
No sound or motion — save over there
A tumble-weed starts on its endless quest
For God knows what — or where.
NELLIE BURGET MILLER

NEITA met me in Denver and took me out to the dry-farming country, where Jack was principal of a large consolidated school, to which came children living within a radius of eight or ten miles. The Careys lived four miles from school and a mile from the nearest neighbor.

From my window I could watch the always changing sky, and over far. horizons and up to our very door the animate tumbleweed in its rhythmic comings and goings. Bright pheasants pranced by, and at night rabbits danced in the moonlight.

The land is rolling prairie, and the landscape unbroken except for fences, windmills, and sometimes on the south side of a farmhouse a few trees, scraggly, windblown, and struggling to live. These trees have been kept alive by patient people, women usually, who have carried numberless pails of water from creaking windmills.

They tell of a family who, in the early days, had no windmill. The husband, who hauled all the water from the farm of a neighbor, refused to bring enough extra to water the few trees and the small flower garden which his wife had carefully planted. So, when her day's work was done, she rolled to the nearest windmill — over a mile away — a large barrel, which she filled with water and then rolled home.

All winter the only change in my health was that at times I was worse. As always, I was eating plenty of nourishing food in a vain effort to keep up my weight, resistance, and strength. It was a long time before I learned — through much suffering, for no doctor ever told me — that this was the worst thing I could do.

Here as elsewhere I had the doctor — he had to come twenty-five miles. He gave me several prescriptions. I've had enough prescriptions in my time to paper a large-sized room, where they would have been more useful than they were for me. I've taken gallons of medicine. I doubt if one drop ever helped me, and some drops, I know, have injured me. Yet tomorrow, if a doctor should write a prescription (and, if there's a doctor around, I'd like to see you prevent him from doing it), I, full of hope and anxious to get my money's worth, would meekly swallow a few doses. The rest would go down the sink.

There are over a million cures, not one universal one. So we asthmatics, grabbing at straws, try the one million. I have inhaled, sniffed, smoked, taken medicine, dieted, and taken a faith cure, all at one and the same time.

It seemed that the wind blew continually, and it was often very cold, with deep snow covering the roads, but fortunately no such blizzard as came the following winter when, on a certain school day as Jack and the children left in the morning, it was cloudy and snowing slightly. As the day advanced, it grew no better. By afternoon it was a young blizzard, heavy snow with a high driving wind. Jack dismissed school and started the busses toward home. The bus that he, his two children, and

many other school children were in, had only
gone a mile or two when it skidded off the
road and refused to start. Jack took the hands
of the two smallest children and put two
large boys at the end of the line. Then, each
one holding on to another, and with heads
down, they breasted that blizzard until, by
going forward a few feet, then turning their
backs and resting, they fought through to a
farmhouse, where they were thawed out. While
they were having supper, one wall of the sod
kitchen blew in, but fortunately none were
injured, and the farmer's wife made beds for
them in a new barn.

Jack telephoned to the various homes that
they were safe — that is, to all but his own.
They had no telephone, and all that bitter
day and night and until ten o'clock the next
day, when a man managed to get a saddle
horse through the drifted snow to tell her,
Neita had been alone. She was terrified by
the terrific wind, the blinding, drifting snow,
tortured by the thought that her husband and
children might be lost in it. I think that to
occupy her mind, and also to keep from running from one window to another, especially

after the snow had drifted over them, she lit the lamp and started in — her only fuel corn-cobs — to cook everything in the house. Anyway, she has written a story about it called, 'Cinnamon and Snow.' I haven't read it, but it ought to be good.

'December 18, '25. A bright warm day. We have made candy and decorated it.'

It's 'Christmas, Christmas in the air, Christmas, Christmas, everywhere.' My room is piled with gaily decorated boxes to be filled with cakes and candy. Earl's and Jose's gifts are ready. Under my bed is a big box containing a Mama doll which, when pressed, sounds like a cat in pain. Neita's room looks as if a whirlwind had gone through an art store. Paper, paints, stickers, cards, and more paper on bed, table, and floor, while under her bed are several mysterious bundles. The kitchen is filled with candies and cakes, also a multitude of unwashed sticky dishes. Down cellar is a tree brought from I don't know where, as it's hundreds of miles to where evergreen trees grow. Also down cellar is a box of oranges, and several buckets of candy for the school treat.

'December 29. Another Christmas, with all its smell, thrills, expectations, and disappointments, has come and gone. With our own and the school preparations it has been a rushing time. Yesterday Jackie, aged five, said, "I wish I was a daddy cow. I would like to butt some people around here." He is a cheerful, faithful nurse. Today he laid a tiny piece of the Christmas tree on the bed beside me saying, "There, Mama-Annie, you can 'tend you are the mother of a baby pine."

'December 31. "The year has gone, and with it many a throng of happy dreams. Its mark is on each brow, its shadow in each heart." And me in bed with a fever of 104! Anyway, I've finished a story, "Prayers are Answered," and I am going to send it to "True Story Magazine." A year from now shall I be here — or there? I don't care. Yes, I do — I do enjoy writing — I want to live and do it.

'February 14. Someone is thankful for "the first sweet smell of rain — rest after pain." Just now I'm thankful for the last part. "Prayers are Answered" returned. It must be pretty bad. The manuscript looks

[142]

as though "True Stories" had used it for a doormat. A red Valentine heart, filled with candy, on my breakfast tray. How I like the little things — or I wonder are the little things really the big things?'

One day each week Neita taught art in the school. On those days Jackie and I would be alone. One sunny noon we took our lunch outside and were eating it in the sheltered corner when a bunch of horses, that had broken their fence and were exulting in their freedom, came tearing down the lane, in through our open gate and up to the windmill. Before I could stop him, Jackie, knowing that the horses getting away would cause their owner no end of trouble, and in order to close the gate, ran among those galloping horses. Too weak to call or go after him, I put my hand over my eyes and went limp.

Then I heard the gate bang and a sturdy 'Get away from there, damn you!'

My eyes opened to see Jackie shooing the horses away from me. I remarked brilliantly, 'Why, Jackie, did I hear you swear?

'Sure you did,' he beamed proudly. 'I know

a lot more swears, too. Want to hear me say 'em? I could whisper 'em in your ear.'

I declined, with thanks. Later that day, before Neita returned, he said, 'Mama-Annie, 'bout swearing. We'll just keep that to ourselves.'

The educational, religious, and social life of this community centered at the schoolhouse and church, built near each other and a mile from the nearest farmhouse. In the basement of the church they had a kitchen outfitted with sufficient dishes, tables, and chairs, for everyone in the community, and scarcely a week passed that there wasn't a gathering either in school or church. Once a month, or oftener, they were visited by county demonstrators, a man to help and advise with the farmer's problems, a woman to help with those of the farmer's wife.

Only once was I able to attend one of these meetings. The demonstrator was a young, attractive college girl. She had with her samples of the things she intended to teach these eager women how to make.

Before this she had written notes to each one in order that they might have their materials with them. She taught them how to make and trim hats, how to make a workable fly trap, how to use bias tape for trimming, and how to make rugs. As they worked, she advised them how to break up a setting hen, how to preserve eggs in water. She stayed all day. At noon the men with their demonstrator came, and the teachers and children from school trooped in. A marvelous dinner was served. What a good, good time! This day the demonstrator also taught the women to make tissue-paper carnations. At this you may smile. I didn't. I know the part that tissue-paper flowers play in the barren lives of some women. I realized it even more when on the following Sunday an enterprising woman brought to church a vase filled with red carnations which, placed on the pulpit, lighted the room and rested the eye. Only paper, yet they had brought to our minds more clearly than the calendar could, or than the preacher had, that it was a day to be remembered — Mother's Day.

With the coming of spring I improved, and another time was able to go to school, where they were having a community picnic. Affairs of this kind, where entire families, from babies to grandparents, meet, visit, play, and break bread together, are wonderful, I think. Bread, however, is a poor name for such marvelous food. Every variety, such quantities, and how we all enjoyed and laughed over everything!

Men were grouped about, talking of things which interested them; young people were giggling secrets; children were everywhere, shouting, running, playing. Women were discussing any and everything. I loved it all, but especially one incident. Rain began to sprinkle. One might think it would not be appreciated at a picnic, but these dry farmers were pleased, for their hopes, their crops, their existence depended on moisture. Then for a few minutes the rain just poured. Men, women, and children ran out, catching it in their hands, on their upturned faces, dancing, splashing in it.

I said to a woman who was returning to shelter, 'You will catch your death in that rain.'

She sang to me, 'It isn't raining rain to me, it's raining a two-door sedan.'

Others took up the refrain. For one it was a

new house, for another her boy going to college, for another the means of going to the hospital for the birth of her baby. One saw wedding clothes, one even decided on a set of false teeth. The men, I think, were mostly concerned with mortgages.

June seventh, after writing in my diary, 'Lady Luck, be good to me,' I left New Haven for Saguache. At this time teeth were supposed to be the cause of every human ill, from falling hair to falling arches. As I will try anything once, I stopped in Sterling and had four perfectly good teeth pulled, which, for a 'noble experiment,' is too many teeth.

In Salida I met Earl, who was working in a store there. After a short visit I went home to spend what I knew would be my last summer in Saguache.

Writing, in so far as I could, I put out of my mind, except for discussing it with two women, both of whom were patient and believing enough not to smile at the idea of my ever becoming an author.

Several days — happy days, because I was doing something — of that last summer stand out in my mind. Were my family or friends writing this, they would say: 'She is foolish. She does things when she knows they will make her ill.' I don't. I do things that make me happy, and I can't bear to admit that my body can rule my spirit.

One day I made cakes for a sister-in-law's party; an angel food, high, wide, and handsome, decorated with scrolls of faintest yellow and green ferns; a spice cake put together with thick creamy chocolate fudge, the top and sides decorated in blending tints of brown. My only tool was a sheet of writing paper rolled into a funnel. Then there was the afternoon when, just to see if I could, I walked up Poncha Pass. Another day when the Boyds took me fishing on the Cochetopa, I slipped away with a blanket and in a sheltered place stripped and took a sunbath. Another time I cooked all day because Earl was coming to see me. Then he telephoned that he had decided to return to Fort Collins instead, work his way, and finish college. I cried with disappointment, and laughed and clapped my hands and danced with happiness.

Before I left that fall, I visited friends in Gunnison, going over the same road I had gone over thirty years before, thinking the same thoughts as then: Where am I going? What am I going to do? Thoughts just as useless now as then. I weighed opportunities. What can I do? What would be best to do? What do I want to do? The last question usually decided the matter, because who knows what he can do or what is best to do? So I, as always, did what I wanted to do, and decided to return to Santa Fé, give myself several months to get well in — which was quite generous of me — and in the meantime rewrite the book.

From Alamosa I went on what we call the 'Chili Line,' a narrow-gauge train running from the San Luis Valley directly to Santa Fé. If you crave travel in foreign places, take this journey. Train crew and passengers are Mexicans. The country through which the train runs, the towns at which it stops, the people at the stations, are all Mexican. The houses along the way are adobe with windows and doors painted a bright blue which I didn't care for until I learned that this color was the blue of heaven, and also a blue symbolizing Mary, the mother of Christ. These houses in the fall are festooned with bright red chili peppers, and all in all it's an engaging picture. If you are like me, you will love this trip, but take along something to eat. You'll need it.

I arrived the day of election. Santa Fé, the capital of New Mexico, is at all times the most interesting town in America, and especially every two years when governor and legislature are elected. The latter is, I think, the only legislative body in the United States where all business is transacted in two tongues, English and Spanish. The outgoing governor gives a reception. He invites everybody and his few remaining friends go. Then the incoming governor gives a reception. Everybody is invited, and everybody goes.

I was mad. Here it was election night in Santa Fé. The last of a battle, a hard fight, and me not able to join the wildly excited crowds filling the streets, the Plaza, and the eating places. Everybody would be there, Mexicans — Mexicans are born politicians — Indians, and Whites. The writers and artists would be out in full force — the artists planning decorations for the inaugural ball, to which everyone but me would go, as the only

[150]

requirements were an evening dress, ten dollars, and a man. The dress, with needle and scissors, I could have managed. The ten dollars, by doing without something else, I could have dug up. But at that time I didn't feel equal to rounding up the man. Later, however, I did see La Fonda's dining-room decorated for the occasion. The walls were entirely covered with short pine and piñon branches, among which at intervals were bunches of glowing poinsettia blossoms. I knew that once Mary Austin and the Cassidys had spent days tying and dyeing, in rainbow tints, bolt upon bolt of cheesecloth to make a decoration for this special occasion.

But I wasn't thinking of a night two months away. I was thinking of this night when successful candidates and friends would, very likely, stage a demonstration both bizarre and brilliant. And to show that they were still in the ring and in two years would be ready for a come-back, the defeated candidates would also swing into the spotlight — I can't remember if that was the time or not when Witter Bynner, tired of taxation without representation, tilted at New Mexico's political windmill.

I do remember, however, that written on doors and gates of artists and writers was 'La Follette, we are here.' And there would be exultation and satisfaction expressed by back-slapping, hand-shaking, and ballyhoo. There would be excuses, alibis, and post-mortems, there would be side-stepping, crawfishing, and a general backing-up to climb on the band wagon.

There would be music and dancing and laughter and gaiety, also much talk in English and very, very much talk in Spanish. In short, it was election night in Santa Fé when I said to myself, 'Oh, well, if I can't do what I want to, I'm going to want to do what I have to. And so to bed.'

'November 4, '26, Santa Fé. I wonder if it is for me "The Land of Journey's Ending"? I am either very brave or simply foolish. Here I am in La Fonda, and am going out in a few minutes to buy me a quilted satin robe. The pocketbook so slim, too! Have called Mary Borrego and think I am going to get a room of hers for ten dollars a month. This accounts for the dressing-gown. If I played safe I would wait and see, but I'm so tired of playing safe.

If I'm any good at all, seems as if I should land a paying job some time in the coming year.'

After a few days I moved to this room in a Mexican's back yard, and after an irritating time was settled and ready to rewrite the book. But somehow I couldn't. I was too ill, too disturbed over finances. I had put myself on a fifty-dollar a month budget, and not many months at that. I was very lonely. Think of being lonely with Edna St. Vincent Millay living not twenty feet away! Were it to do over I'd write a note, 'For God's sake, Edna, come over and see me.' And I bet she would. Mary Austin did come and brought home-made apple jelly and a rose geranium leaf in the glass.

CHAPTER XIII

God! Give me hills to climb and strength for climbing.
                                        ARTHUR GUITERMAN

AFTER Thanksgiving I was much worse and called a doctor, who came, gave me a look, sat nonchalantly down, lit a cigarette and asked me if he might smoke. I don't know whether he was addressing me as a Victorian or as an asthmatic. From the first I liked him and wrote in my diary:

'December 10, Saint Vincent's Hospital. Been here three or four days. Doctor brought me. It is unusual for me to have this sort of doctor — one who is interested and wants to cure me, not merely relieve me.'

There was a lot about the doctor that I wrote in no diary. I don't trust diaries with everything. I was building the most wonderful air castles with him as the *motif*. Poor thing, he never knew that he had fallen desperately in love with me and had coaxed me to marry him and that I, much against my will, had finally consented and we were married. Our clothes, food, house, furnishings — everything was all worked out in detail. He was a bachelor whose house and offices were already tastefully furnished, but women being what they are, I, in my mind, changed everything. In my diary I wrote only this:

'As the winds of chance lift the fabric of life from the seamy side, I catch glimpses of a lovely right side.

'December 13, Saint Vincent's. Too many Sunday accidents and Doctor too busy to take me home. Have just been out of bed toe-dancing on rug, always my first expression of being better. I am also enough better to have stopped dreaming about Doctor (poor, simple, lonely, old fool!) — I like Doctor. I like the sisters and envy everyone the busy day yesterday. How I want to be in the thick of things!

'December 14, Saint Vincent's. I'm going home today. Another night, and I think more clearly and have come to this conclusion. I have been thinking too much about myself, have, in fact, been indulging in self-pity, which is something I hate in anyone, most of all in myself. Impressions over ten days. Letting go and resting. Trying to show off before Doctor. I mean talking — that is the form my showing off takes. Bed-baths leaving me wet, especially around neck. Flowers from Mrs. Taylor, good meals, stormy weather, cars coming at night over Hill of the Martyrs back of Moorish Shriners' Temple, people going in and out of Colonial Court House. Buzzers for nurses, sweet-faced sisters, click of billiard balls. [This irritated and worried me. I feared I was out of my head, for of course there could be no billiard-room in a hospital. But there was.] Children's voices singing. Cathedral bells and black-shawled Mexican women coming through the snow to early mass. Waiting for Doctor, planning clever things to say to him. Dreadful weakness and sweats — yes, sweats. I don't perspire — I sweat. Watching stars at night, longing and reaching out and longing for I don't know what. Mexican and Indian nurses. The Indians have the Indian sign on me. A feeling, when I leave anything on my tray, what a shame, with one hundred and sixty orphans right in the yard. I have never been so close to an orphanage before. Lovely furnished rooms, not at all like a hospital, and efficiency, service, and help. Doctor says I've been very sick. I don't think so. He should see me when I've really been under the weather.

'December 31, '26. Been home ever since December 17. Left Saint Vincent amid smiles and tears, me furnishing both. Not very well. Mary builds my fires and lifts ashes. If I should make the year's recapitulation, it would be something like this (only I shouldn't do it tonight. I'm too let down): Five months in bed, not including nights, coughing at least two hours each of these nights. Any one of the nights, I believe, I should have been less tired to have had a baby. Each day and night fighting cold. A few lovely days in Saguache, especially the day I made Hallie's cakes. (If I could only be able to work, for when I work I sing.) Counting my money, wondering where to go. But what's the use? I should be thankful things are no worse, and that my family are all right. Well, I am, but, oh, I want either to live or die. Beginning to-morrow I'm going to try and write some each day. Here I sit in my bathrobe, my feet on a hot-water bottle, a rattle in my throat.

'"Anne, I wish you a happy New Year."'

One cold, raw day I was sitting wrapped to the eyebrows in the ell of the house in the weak sunshine while a Mexican neighbor's hungry, nervous, high-hipped cow, in a fruitless search for food, crowded by me countless times. I wrote in the diary:

'January 6, '27. I'm like Walt Whitman when he says,

> "And I say to mankind
> Be not curious about God.
> For I who am curious about each
> Am not curious about God."

(No array of terms can say how much I am at peace with God and calm about death.)'

Below this I wrote, and I don't know whether it was to show Walt that I too could write poetry or what, but anyway it shows what a grab bag my mind is:

> I do not care why, with whom,
> Or where Aimee went.
> Much vital more to me is this,
> How can I pay my rent?

> Did or did not Mrs. Hall
> Kill her husband's friend?
> I do not care; this means much more to me,
> Where will my asthma end?

Will skirts be short or long?
I do not care.
This is the burden of my song;
To have at once new spring underwear.

Is Governor Dillon fine or bum,
I do not care.
Much more to me is this —
Why doesn't the doctor come?

Early in January, the doctor insisted that I go to a nursing home. After counting assets — two Liberty bonds and the rent on my house in Saguache — I found that I could go for a few months only. By now I had given up writing and spoke of my manuscript hesitatingly, shamedly. The doctor and nurse were kind, and did everything in their power for me, but I grew no better. I saw no future and really wanted to die. I even considered suicide, and refrained only because I will not let life down me and will never consciously bring trouble or disgrace to my family.

That spring, Jack gave up his position in Colorado and decided to live in Arizona so that I, who needed a warmer climate, could live with them.

They came to Santa Fé for the summer, and it was a long hard summer for all of us. The

[159]

Careys were moving, there was no job in sight, I was very ill and hopeless — I, who have always been my family's hope-giver.

One day after the Cassidys had just returned from Europe, Neita went to call, and because they had praised my book she returned home all enthusiastic. They told her that the editor had also praised it and that when the form was changed it was reasonably sure of publication.

This was new life to me, I planned how to go about changing it, but never started. Later Mrs. Cassidy urged me to begin. I doubted if I could write.

'Besides,' I told her, 'I am going to die.'

She jumped up and snapped, 'Damn it all, if you've decided to die, go on then and die.'

Which is just the kind of bedside manner I like. It should be used often and universally. Instead of dying, I started to write.

The high light of that summer was the Fiesta, a clever, colorful celebration where everyone enters into the spirit and gaiety of the occasion. It was maddening for me not to be able to take in all of the Fiesta. However, I did see streets and plazas much decorated, and buildings strung with many electric lights. Each bulb was covered with an ordinary paper bag to soften the light. I saw everybody in either Spanish or Indian costume. Many of the natives wore wonderful clothes handed down from generation to generation.

The preceding evening I saw people climbing the Hill of Martyrs where, near the large cross, lit only by bonfires sending up wraith-like wisps of smoke, priests impressively sanctioned and blessed the forthcoming celebration.

I saw everyone, and I mean everyone, irrespective of class, creed, or station, mingled on the streets and Plaza visiting, singing, dancing, rubbing elbows, and acting in a gay 'When you knows everybody and they all knows you' manner.

I saw the joyful burning of a huge figure, fashioned by the artists and named, 'Dull Care.'

I saw the camp where hundreds of Indians were provided for during the Fiesta. Cooks were hired to prepare the food which was served at long tables set up in the open. In this camp were Indians and their families of all ages, hailing from several different pueblos. They all ate together, but otherwise each pueblo stayed in its own group. They necessarily lived in very close quarters. But in spite of this, and in spite of the pueblos competing against each other for the six days they were camped in Santa Fé (city of Holy Faith), there was not one word of dissension, one cry from a single child, one complaint, excuse, or lament from a solitary dancer.

I saw some of the pueblo governors with their baton of authority — a silver-headed cane which had been presented to former governors by President Abraham Lincoln.

I saw the Hysterical Parade in which beauty and farce were intermingled. A bull-fight was staged in front of Governor Dillon's box — a two-by-four — over which a Spanish shawl was draped. The men rode burros instead of horses, the rider's feet often resting on the ground. The bull, very much on the prod and bellowing and pawing the air, was a head and hide fitted over a frame, with two men supplying the inner works and motive power. Gustave Bauman, noted etcher, very realistically took the part of the tail end.

I saw Billy-the-Kid dramatized on top of La Fonda. The actors — local people in the dance-hall — were drinking real drinks, tempting and tantalizing the spectators.

I attended the Conquistadores Ball. Something special. Society, notables, clothes, such clothes, and shawls — *real* Spanish shawls — and the most dignified gentleman I saw there was, in my opinion, the Toas Indian Tony Luhan, dancing with the daughter-in-law of his white wife, Mabel Luhan.

I saw the pageant staged in an out-of-doors theater and at the cost of much money, time, and labor. The numerous trappings, costumes, and people represented everything except, as Benchley once said, 'Three hard-boiled eggs.'

A man on either side of the bowl interpreted its meaning, one in English, the other in musical Spanish. It was really beautiful and impressive, although not comparable to the Indian dances.

In the pageant Neita represented Gold. The actors were so thinly clad that, when the prospector discovered her and she sprang to her feet, exclaiming, 'I am Gold,' one didn't know whether she was saying, 'I am cold,' or

'I am bold.' In fact, the principal actors and dancers were all unduly unclothed, or so thought the actual priests taking part in the play. An indignant costume-maker and assistants had to sit up an entire night making slips and dyeing underwear.

Oh, the Indian dances, how really wonderful they are, with their accompaniment of music! They are the most stirring, thrilling spectacle I've ever witnessed. I won't attempt to describe the Corn Dance, the Eagle Dance, the Comanche War Dance, but only the Deer Dance, which won first place. And now I am unable to describe the catch in my throat from the time I caught a first glimpse of antlered heads climbing in single file up a steep path. Then, unhurried, to the chanting of music and the throbbing of drums, the body of the deer, moving in perfect rhythm, came into view. They were so realistic as to be breath-taking, but were Indians naked except for a breech-cloth, to which was fastened a short tail and green piñon boughs. On each head was fastened, so securely that one might think they had grown there, a deer's many-pointed antlers. In each hand the Indian had a stick which, decorated in piñon, composed his front legs. During the entire dance the Indians did not straighten up, but, bent over, the heavy horns carried proudly, easily on their heads, they went through intricate steps and movements symbolically portraying the life of a deer or man from birth to death. And to think that a few years ago there were unseeing people who wanted to, and almost did, pass a law prohibiting these dances!

In September the Careys went to Phoenix. I was to follow as soon as they were settled, although I didn't want to, for my own sake, for their sakes, and for the sake of peace. I didn't want to live with my children. Life was hard enough for them without my adding to the burden. I was going, nevertheless, cheerfully and as gracefully as I could, when Fate, in the shape of my friend Julia Armstrong, took a hand. She urged me to accept help from her until I could regain my health. This I did gladly, sorrowfully, shamedly and very, very gratefully.

Before leaving I saw the doctor and asked his bill for services rendered — services covering one year, when he gave me of his skill and

[165]

time, including numerous day and night calls, weeks of light treatments at his office, countless hypodermics in a vain effort to build up my resistance, medicine, fluoroscopes, X-rays, and best of all, a keen wit and ready tongue which kept me striving for a ready come-back and mentally on the jump.

I expected to pay for all of this sometime, and knew that it would run into hundreds of dollars. I'd done some worrying, too. So when I made my farewell visit I said, 'By the way Doctor' — isn't it absurd how we say 'by the way' as a preface to things which have been filling our days and nights, blotting out the horizon? — 'now that I think of it, what is the amount of my bill?'

My jaw was set, my hands were clenched, as I waited for his answer. He reached over and patted my shoulder.

'Young lady, he said, 'that bill is ready and waiting and I shall expect payment' — he hesitated and looked my frail frame up and down — 'on the day that you weigh two hundred pounds.'

Tears burned in my eyes. I couldn't thank him. I choked as I went through the door, and flung to him over my shoulder something flippant.

I had rewritten the book, and it was almost typed — by whom do you suppose? Olive! Yes, Olive, who had become well enough to leave the sanitarium and take a business course and who was now a full-fledged stenographer. I was pleased when she wrote me that she was hampered in typing because she had to stop so often to laugh. But Olive's was a free-and-easy laughter, and later I learned that it was caused not altogether by my humor, but partly by my fantastic spelling and punctuation.

I stayed two days in Albuquerque to rush her on the final typing. The evening I started south for Phoenix, the manuscript started east for New York.

CHAPTER XIV

When life is more terrible than death,
it is the truest valor to live.

SIR THOMAS BROWNE

ALBUQUERQUE is where I should have stayed,
but next on my list of cures was climate, a warm
one, and Phoenix was supposed to turn the
trick.

I arrived in a cold rain and went directly
to what was supposedly one of the best
sanitariums in the city. The buildings in
front were imposing, but cottages, comforts,
and prices decreased as one receded toward
the back of the lot.

I, of course, was at the extreme end, next
to the chicken-coop and incinerators, and
paid twenty-three dollars a week. The best
rooms were, I understood, fifty dollars a week.
My cottage was ten by twelve, built part way
up of one layer of boards. It was open all
around, with canvas flaps to keep out cold and
wind. In addition to a small built-in clothes
closet, the complete furniture consisted of a
high, narrow hospital bed, which may be easier

for a nurse but which is quite otherwise for the patient, one kitchen chair, three home-made drawers on which a small mirror rested, and in one corner a shelf which supported a white enamel basin and pitcher. Under the shelf was a slop-jar.

I soon found that the attitude toward sick people was quite different from that in New Mexico. Here they were set apart and somehow made to feel their illness more. I don't know just how to explain this. I want to be fair. Perhaps I can do it best by saying that Albuquerque advertises itself as the health city of the world and tries to live up to the advertisement. Phoenix advertises itself as a winter resort, and also, in spite of the hundreds of people flocking there seeking health in its glorious sunshine, tries to carry on as advertised.

The food at this sanitarium was marvelous in quality, quantity, and preparation. There was a charming young nurse who fluttered her eyelids at the men as a female bird does its wings, and probably for the same reason.

Each evening the doctor made his rounds. He was a handsome man who chewed tobacco incessantly and, in spite of signs forbidding it, expectorated to the right and left. You could see him like a glow-worm coming through the night, carrying a tray on which was a burning alcohol lamp to sterilize the thermometer, also several kinds and colors of pills and tablets. One could imagine him in pre-Volstead days saying, 'Come on. What will be yours? Name your poison.'

As always when I made a new move, the weather was unusual. It was now cold and rainy, and I was very miserable. People would wander in from the street and look in at us in bed as though we were caged animals.

One day a woman, after staring at me several minutes, said cheerfully, 'Aren't you dreadfully lonely in there?'

I, who was just then bringing up all my reserve forces in order to keep a stiff upper lip!

There was no spirit of friendliness in either doctor, nurses, or patients. My nearest neighbor was a very sick young girl. She never looked my way, never spoke, but at night I could hear her softly crying and calling, 'Mama, mama.' I asked if I could do anything, but she didn't hear me. She was dreaming.

Every rainy day to lessen the cold — but it didn't — they brought into my room an oil stove that smoked. This smoke and the smoke and stench which came from the rubbish and bone-burning incinerator, added to the 'good wholesome food' which the doctor insisted that I eat, made my asthma rampant, so I 'Wandering Jewed' it to another sanitarium out on the desert.

These moves were not so easy as they sound. I loathe moving and never do it without sleepless nights.

For days Jack and Neita looked for a suitable, not too expensive, place, which they finally found some miles from Phoenix. It was run by an honest, hard-working, kindly family who knew very little about running a sanitarium. For nineteen dollars a week I had a small, nicely furnished room, two sides of which were open with canvas flaps. There was no heat, no bath, no hot water except that brought from the kitchen over a hundred feet away. In this cottage were two other rooms, one occupied by a girl who had almost made

the cure, the other by a woman lying quietly
day after day with a bag of shot on her lung.
These shot-bags are made of heavy ticking
filled with shot. Some of them weigh several
pounds and are used to collapse the lung.
Neither patients nor proprietors seemed to
have any idea of sanitation or the danger of
infection. Patients were in and out of the
kitchen, helping with the preparation of food,
using the telephone, and the same bathroom.
In short, it was run just as one would run a
boarding-house for well people.

Only once did I eat in the dining-room, and
that time, as the saying goes, I 'broke my
plate' by talking too much. None of the
patients were particularly well-bred, and this
day at dinner only talked of cures and cavities,
lungs or the lack of them. I stood it as long
as I could, but when the life of the party, a
smart Alex, said something pertaining to
'bugs,' I cried out, 'Can't you talk about anything else?'

Whereupon he said, 'We've all got the bug
here so we talk about it. As a newcomer, just
what would you care to discuss?'

And I, weak and trembling, couldn't think

[172]

of a thing but 'companionate marriage,' which shocked them much more than 'bugs' had shocked me.

The desert was really beautiful. From my bed, through the open flap, I could see many grayish-green trees and plants, all new to me — ironwood, graceful palo verde. A fluted-columned saguaro, almost animate in its individuality, cheered and strengthened me for each new day.

At night, in order to forget such pressing worries as my health, Earl struggling at school, and the Careys living in a two-room house with no job in sight, I would think of old songs or try to remember poetry. Sometimes I thought of pleasant words like health, home, happy, humor, heaven, husband; or of pleasant conditions such as independence, security, sleep, warmth, peace; or of beauty — leaves dancing in the moonlight, columbines glinting through aspen trees, sunsets, a freshly scrubbed floor, and even a bunch of tissue-paper roses pinned many, many years before on a freshly hung curtain.

The carpenter who was building new cottages resented being called from his work to carry trays and wait upon women in bed. It was also his duty to bring the mail, which he did in a very haphazard manner. Perhaps I thought so just because he brought me none.

Those were miserable months, and if it had not been for Neita's visits I doubt if I could have stood them. I met few of the patients and didn't want to meet them. The most interesting person there, I thought, was a poor broken-down Jew, whom everyone but me shunned. He spoke broken English and was very hard to understand, but he read and thought and was worth listening to. His visits, however, always left me limp, for his had been such a trouble-filled life and I could see no hope nor help for him. Some Jewish organization was giving him a small amount to live on, and most of this, I think, went for tobacco.

At any hour in the night I would be awakened by a pungent pipe smell. It would be Cohen, unable to sleep from pain, walking, walking and thinking his restless thoughts. But that shattered piece of humanity told me one of the sweetest love stories I've ever heard.

It is difficult to find words to write Cohen's story, which, because of his illness, he whispered to me. Then, too, so much of it I did not get from mere words, but from the shrug or straightening of drooped shoulders or from the wringing of long-fingered, sensitive hands, from a wetness in troubled eyes, or, at rare intervals, from the shadow of a happy, wistful smile.

Born in northern Russia, his earliest memories were of existing, like a sparrow, on what food he could pick up from the floor or tables in the various eating-places. Being so young, he could walk under the tables without touching his head.

Thus he grew up, never experiencing any of the better things in life. Somehow he learned to read and to design women's clothes.

Finally, uneducated, uncouth, he arrived in Paris, where he found work.

One day his employer sent him to the home of a rich customer, for whose daughter Cohen was to design a trousseau. Never before had he seen anyone like her. I wish I might describe in his words her loveliness, beauty, charm, and graciousness. From the first moment he saw her he loved her with a love deep, everlasting. He was overpowered, consumed with a life's love, which might have been divided among

[175]

parents, home, relatives, and friends, but which now centered on her.

Knowing that she was not for him, he tried to put her out of his mind. Still, every waking moment she was before him — her smile, her voice, the turn of her head. His nights were filled with dreams of her. For hours at night he would walk the streets, always unintentionally ending up in front of her home. Relentlessly he fought with himself, swearing that he would down his feeling and forget her, only to find himself making business excuses for her to come to the shop or for him to go to her home.

On one of these occasions, when, silently and tremblingly he was fitting her, her hand without warning fell on his bent head, and she asked, 'Why do you tremble so?'

Cohen stammered words that meant, 'But you could never care for me.'

Well, it seemed that she could, and did. All his life this had been a wonder to Cohen. He didn't see how she could.

At once, with Matell managing everything, they eloped and were married and came to New York, where he, determined to give his wife a small part of the things she had given up, plunged into work.

He was very successful and in time had a fine apartment, beautifully and artistically furnished. They had no friends and wanted none. Matell would have no maid. She herself did the cooking, planning things to please him, making a ceremony of each meal, decorating and serving the food in the manner she had been accustomed to. Each evening both dressed for dinner, and afterwards they read and studied or had music. Matell eagerly teaching, Cohen, an apt scholar, eagerly learning.

Each evening, on his return from work, he brought her a gift. In turn she always had a surprise for him. He dwelt on the colors and richness of the many silk pajamas she made and monogrammed for him.

One evening her surprise was the announcement that they were to have a baby.

This rounded out their happiness, which lasted until the child was five years old, when both it and Matell became ill with diphtheria and died. Cohen died then too, in a way, I think.

Each day my health was worse. I dreaded

the nights, but the days were no better. Once, as I whistled to keep up my courage, I said to my neighbor, 'Hear that bird? He seems to sing, "Prett-ee soon, prett-ee soon." That means that soon we shall be better.'

Thereupon the woman, unimaginative, secure, replied, 'I only hear the dove that goes, "No-o hope, no-o hope."'

One day I thought a bath might brighten life so that again I could see through rose-colored glasses. In the morning I suggested it to Mrs. Aimes. She said if she could find time she would heat the water. When Mr. Aimes came with breakfast, I asked him if he would bring over the washtub. He would, he said, when he got around to it. I waited impatiently because, when one has decided on a bath, after months of waiting, one wants it right away. Still I waited, but nothing happened. As evening came, I went to the door and yelled for water. Nothing happened. By this time I was a nervous wreck, but determined to have a bath, I called to a small boy that I wanted to see Mr. and Mrs. Aimes at once. The latter was really a lovely woman, although worked to death. The former can best be described by his own question when I showed him a picture of Earl, who was graduating that spring, in cap and gown. 'What is he, anyway,' he asked, 'a sailor?' Finally a tin tub was thrown against my door, and a tea kettle of hot water set inside, while Mr. Aimes called sarcastically,

'There you are. Guess that will be all you will want for twenty minutes, anyway.'

'No,' I replied sweetly, 'I thought you at least would come in and wash my back.'

The day before Christmas I was out-of-doors sitting in the sun, an apparently inert bundle of a woman placidly basking; but inside of me a battle was raging. Every sensible force was fighting desperately because it knew it just had to win against the rebellion which attacked it; against the self-pity which must be crushed; against the despair which must be conquered. All this I realized fully. Yet the spirit of right was losing ground, forced to the wall by resentment and hardness. Suddenly came a sound of jingling sleigh-bells, of voices singing Christmas carols! This — on the desert — at midday, with a bright sun blazing down! The battle was lost. Good and right thinking were defeated. Now to cap everything I had lost my mind.

Then around the corner whizzed a truck, gaily decorated in Christmas greens and filled with singers, one of whom was dressed as Santa Claus. There were also numerous packages piled in the truck.

It seems that a few years before a man who was suffering with tuberculosis spent one lonely Christmas on the desert where he made his cure. When Christmas came again, he, with an understanding heart, shared his cheer and gifts with as many as possible. This had grown into a club, so large that each Christmas every health-seeker on the desert had a box which contained fruit, home-made jelly, cake, candy, nuts, and also a personal message.

After singing 'Holy night, silent night,' which always affects me, Santa Claus came to where I sat and, with a 'Merry Christmas,' handed me a brightly decorated box. I didn't raise my head. I never spoke. I couldn't. I was choked, blinded by tears which ran down my face, dripped to the ground; tears that cleared my vision and washed away the lump from my throat, the hardness from my heart.

CHAPTER XV

Oh, gods! if there be any gods, lift me
to your never lonely kingdom.

YOUNGHILL KANG

'CHRISTMAS night, 1927. The end of a perfect
day. In the first place, Jack has landed a
school. I'm so glad. Early this A.M. I was
startled to find on my doorknob a huge stock-
ing filled with numerous gifts, each wrapped as
only Neita can wrap them. It seems that last
night after I was in bed she and Jack came and
left it. I then opened gifts from Earl, Jose, and
Olive — all lovely. Later Jack came and took
me to town. A beautiful drive. Central
Avenue a nine-mile bower of bending trees.
Today the road was richly covered with yellow
leaves looking like dancing twenty-dollar gold
pieces. Neita's decorations were eye and soul
satisfying. More gorgeous and tasteful gifts —
a down quilt, if you please — a good dinner,
then I rested upstairs. Evening back to desert,
where we all had a fine Christmas dinner
served in my room and eaten on boxes, chairs,
the bed, and floor. The Careys have gone, and
I to bed, tired and happy.

'December 31. Nine at night. Only a few more hours of 1927 — what has it meant to me? No better in health. Not very good financially. I'm in debt for the first time in years. More patience and sense. More faith in myself. What will 1928 bring? This I hope — health or better health. I will do the rest.

'February 6. When I arrived here I decided not to tell them I was a writer. When word came about my book, as I knew it soon would, I intended to declare myself and startle them. Gosh! I am the surprised one. Never one word. I was prepared for its return, not for this eating silence. A patient told me our troubles and sufferings are God's way of bringing us into the channel planned for us. I can't believe it of God. Still — if the book is ever published and does any good it will be because of asthma. Have been reading Harry Lauder's "Roamin' in the Gloamin'," where he tells about his son being killed in the war. That war was a loss to everyone. When we wonder what is the matter with times, people, and politics, we should remember that the best, the ones who today would be leaders, were killed or ruined. Next war I suggest drafting the physically and mentally unfit. Criminals ought to make fine fighting material.

'February 24. I'm sick. The 22nd went to town to Snake Indian Dance (hope Neita never finds out). Open car, windy and cold. Crouched and held hat on. Had to be helped up steps. Dances not good after Santa Fé, although they do their stuff with snakes, hundreds of them. Audience not enthusiastic and maddened me with their fun-making. They seemed to think the Indians were stunting for their amusement, not realizing that every movement, every feather, was symbolical.

'Thank God I'm able to dream again, hopeful, constructive day-dreams. While I have been sick I have at times looked back over my life and found it empty because I could not, through misery, see the dreams with which all the years have been filled. Just now I'm beginning to make my aircastles stronger, and my ships are upon the sea.'

I knew I should go to another sanitarium, but was just too weak to make the effort. Then a woman in town who wanted patients heard of me and took me to her place, but I wanted to go to a sanitarium where there was a doctor in attendance.

After repeated endeavors and with the help of friends, Neita arranged an appointment with the head doctor of a sanitarium which had always a long waiting list. As he was a very fine doctor, we sat in the office with renewed hope, waiting to see him.

Many others were waiting — men and women, all young, some dressed in street clothes, many in bathrobes.

They sat expectantly, talking in hushed voices, their eyes fastened upon the doctor's door. All at once that door swung open and he made a dramatic entrance. No, not entrance. He just stood there and received the silent admiration of his patients, who slipped forward in their seats and fairly beamed upon him. I was impressed and when our turn came almost trembled in my eagerness to be a patient of his.

He told us crisply to be seated. Just as crisply he told us that there was a waiting list, and inquired just why I was so anxious to get into this particular sanitarium. I told him first because of the price — twenty dollars per week, which covered everything. It was,

moreover, a wonderful, up-to-the-minute sanitarium, and he was a noted doctor who per-
formed miraculous cures. It was, in a way, my
last hope.

He listened attentively. Then he asked for
the history of my case.

I started my patter. I've repeated it so
many times to so many different doctors that
I can reel it off. All was going well until I came
to the place where my asthma started. At the
word 'asthma' the doctor swung around.

'Have you asthma?'

Then, not waiting for a reply, he added, very
crisply, 'There is no need of taking up more
time. No asthmatic can come in here.'

He rose to show that the call was over.

In desperation I asked, 'What am I to do,
then?'

He said, 'That's your problem, not mine.'

Hard-boiled, I thought.

Well, so can I be hard-boiled, too, and now I
foolishly threw down the gauntlet. 'I bet I do
get in here. There are wires I can pull.'

'It will be over my dead body,' he answered,
just as foolishly.

Here Neita's calm voice broke in.

'Dr. ——, we are strangers here. Could you not tell us of a good nursing home?'

He could and did. Also before we left he made an appointment for me to come back to his sanitarium for food tests and X-rays, and instructed the nurse to charge it to 'charity.' How that word cut and burned!

I hadn't asked for charity. If twenty dollars a week has to be added to by charity, it shouldn't be so. Things should be changed, or what are we people in ordinary circumstances to do?

I went to this small sanitarium, efficiently managed by a nurse, where I paid twenty-three dollars a week. Bed patients not able to wait on themselves paid twenty-five a week. The Methodist Sanitarium is the only place I know of where every service is included in the price named, whether it be fifty or ninety dollars a month.

The nurse was very good and would take me to Dr. ——'s sanitarium for various tests. Each time we went he threw his door wide with the same dramatic gesture. Each time patients glowed and smiled, while I thought resentfully, 'Too bad you all haven't tails to wag.'

'March 16. Borah thinks Republicans should return Sinclair money. So do I. He in turn should give it to me to build a hospital for asthma ailers. This would clean that tainted tin. I've been reading "Why We Behave like Human Beings." When Mrs. B. was making my bed I told her about it. She was hurt and a little peeved to think that I would read about evolution. She is a wonderfully sweet, religious woman, whose religion has upheld her through sixty-one years of almost unbearable trouble and defeat. She said that she could not go on if it were not for her beliefs. I wonder if we who are not sure and who have no belief except that of right living are to be praised for going on through trouble-filled lives, wishing that there might be a heaven but doubting it. This matter of evolution is such a long complicated performance. How much easier, if you could believe, to take dust and a rib and finish the job at once.

'April 1. As I sit here in bed I can see my cheeks cave in. It is hard to keep my courage and I must often say as Lincoln did, "This too shall pass away." Why this fight of nature to keep alive? My mind or spirit would rather

[187]

give up. But each day I learn something from the workers around me. I supposed that I had courage, but I find I haven't a "patchin" on some others. I thought I had faith, hope, and charity. I have, but nothing in comparison to others. I supposed I was long on guts and strength; each day I hear of women to whom I couldn't hold a candle. I have flattered myself that I was good, capable, a worker, a cook, a manager; and I find I'm not in it. I thought I had troubles; now I find that, compared to others, I was having a picnic. One has to be sick to find these good-hearted, patient women.'

From one, without her knowing it, for she was no whiner, I gathered that life had handed her a rough deal. Her relatives, husband, and children had leaned on her until age and illness had taken their toll, when like a worn-out garment she was thrown aside.

To her patients she was not only a nurse, but a wise, cheerful, helpful mother as well, and, in spite of receiving a very small salary, she never made a trip to town but she brought each a small gift — a package of gum, or an orange, or postcard, or newspaper. To do this was against rules, so she secretly slipped the gift to each patient, making him think he was the favored one.

Here was another, an old, old lady working, making beds, sweeping, dusting for sick people, and so sweet, cheerful, and linnet-like as she chirruped and hopped around that one might think she had never known sorrow.

One day, when she was singing 'Mary out on the wild moor,' I told her that my mother used to sing that song. Whereupon, although she had very little time and it was against rules, she dropped everything and we visited. She told of work, of bitter hardship, of poverty — not complaining, mind you, but as though it had been a happy time, and one which she would like to relive. She told of four of her five children being sick at the same time with scarlet fever, and of how for over a month she was the only one to nurse them, and so sleepy and tired that she would cling to the wall and bed in order to keep on her feet. One by one they had died. 'But,' she said, 'I thank the good God that he spared Rosie.' She told of the death of her husband, and that although there had been only thirty dollars for funeral expenses, a kind undertaker had made this amount do for everything. 'Even to a nice suit and shirt, and lovely black tie, and he [the husband] looked quite like he did in his younger days. And just the other evening I was looking at the sunset — you may think I was dreaming, but I wasn't — when right in the sky something like a window opened and himself with the children looked through the window and waved their hands and smiled at me.'

Once a meek, elderly maid who was telling me of the glories of her small rose garden and shack on the desert, went on to say that before she came West she had lived in a large manufacturing city where she herself was one of the cogs in the numerous wheels, and although her health broke, she kept on working. She wanted money to give her husband, whose love, she knew, had grown cold. She knew he was having an affair with another woman, but she never reproached him. Then one day he brought her a pair of old shoes, saying he had found them on the dump-pile. It was raining, but she noticed the shoes were dry.

The next day a neighbor said to her: 'Why

do you stand for it? Rosalene has better clothes for every day than you have for church.'

The meek one asked, 'Has Rosalene new shoes?'

Rosalene had. It was the last straw. Then the meek one got those shoes, set them square in the middle of friend husband's pillow, packed her clothes, and without a backward glance walked out on him.

This one was old, uneducated, and rather crude, but clean inside and out. Life for her had always been hard, but she didn't know it. The years had boosted her from one place to another, until now she was a maid in a sanitarium, where, in order to hold her job, she was required to do the work of several. She would sweep, dust, and scrub the cottages and wash dishes and carry trays. And with all the hurry, rush, and run, she found time to tuck a flower in her gray hair. I watched her from my bed and saw that at every meal-time, when she came along the walk by the flowers, she snapped off a sweet pea and placed it on each tray.

On a certain day I was to be fluoroscoped with ten or twelve other patients. We were herded like sheep into a dark room, where we huddled while one at a time each groped her way to the machine and stepped upon a platform. The only light was the eerie one which enveloped her bare chest, and through which Dr. —— looked into the innermost recesses of her body. Reading quickly, he snapped his findings to a nurse who took it all down.

Only two of these reports did I understand. To one girl he said, 'You are all right. Get out of here and get a job.' Hope ran through the group in happy gurgles, low laughs, whispers of congratulations. To the other he said, 'It's two months in bed for you.' She stepped off with an audible 'Damn.'

My turn came. I walked on and was greeted with 'What the hell? Get off there and get out of whatever it is you have on.' Someone, through the darkness, reached a hand to me, and I leaned against a bare body while the offending slip which I, being Victorian, had kept on, was dropped from my shoulders.

Since for weeks I had been unable to walk without someone to hold on to, this performance finished me. I had no more than reached the waiting-room when I keeled over, but not exactly in a faint because my spirit was still there. (Recently I fainted in the dining-room of the Los Angeles Biltmore, when my spirit did, for a short time, go away somewhere while my body relaxed in a most exquisite rest.) I was tired of fighting, and as I wilted on the floor I hoped that I'd break a leg or something so that they would put me to bed and I never need arise.

A nurse lifted me on a stretcher. I smiled inwardly, thinking, 'I've got the best of him. I bet this is a stroke and I'll have to stay in his old san.' Although I was apparently unconscious, my senses were still working, so that I took in every detail while two nurses ministered to me. Within the hour I revived — just my luck — and was hustled off home.

I like doctors, not because of their profession, which is undoubtedly the noblest one, but because they are very human, interesting, and entertaining men. Usually they like me, and when they enter my cottage they let down, light a cigarette and we visit; but not Dr. ——. He was always dignified, always professional.

Dr. —— instructed my nurse that twice a

day I was to stand on my head. This was a
new one, but I tried my best. I would move to
the edge of the bed and slip out until my head
rested on the floor, then the nurse put an iron-
ing-board against the foot of the bed and
helped me to get placed so that I lay with my
head downhill. It was not a success, and re-
sulted in copious nose-bleeds.

The next week, when the Doctor was preparing to give me a hypodermic, he asked,
'Have you been standing on your head?'

'Now, Doctor, have a heart!' I pleaded.
'When I can't even stand on my feet, how in
the world do you expect me to stand on my
head? Besides, it gives me dreadful nose-
bleeds.'

'You are not following instructions,' he said
crisply. 'Lowering the head very often helps
to drain the tubes.' (Doctor, of course, used
medical terms, unspellable by me.)

'But, Doctor,' I cried out, 'can't you do
something for me so that there will be nothing
to drain?'

At this he threw the hypodermic, into which
he was fitting a needle, one direction, the
needle another, and stalked out, saying, as he

went, 'You and I seem to be working at cross-purposes.'

I grew no better. Phoenix was getting hot. I was tired of the struggle. I decided to return to New Mexico to die.

'May 1, '28. At six P.M. I leave for New Mexico. Not happy, but contented. I know now I am to climb no heights, realizing after being in the depths that there is a simple middle place where I could be very happy if I could only sleep at night, breathe, and work during the day and, to round out the cup, have a home on a hillside.'

CHAPTER XVI

Science and philosophy, theaters and books, seem tame in comparison with men and women.

LINCOLN STEFFENS

I WENT directly to the Methodist Sanitarium, where they graciously welcome an incoming, and just as graciously speed an outgoing, guest. But Ma, dear Ma, was not there to greet me. She had gone — 'Over the range,' as we Westerners say. Sometime before she returned from a hospital, where she had had an operation, to go on duty at the sanitarium, she was called by one of her old patients who was dying. She got out of bed and worked through the night with him, and in the morning they went away together.

Hope springing eternal in an asthmatic's breast, I employed a doctor who when he came wanted, of course, to examine me for T.B. I told him that I had had numerous tests, all negative, all expensive. He smiled, and let it be known that he took no doctor's decisions other than his own.

'It's queer,' I said, 'that we, the patients, are supposed to take as gospel each and every doctor's report, when you in the profession will not take those of each other.' A patient who had 'chased' for years once told me that she had grown so accustomed to tests that the moment she saw a doctor she started involuntarily to bare her chest.

He made the examination with me, 'Ahing' and 'ninety-nining' to the tune of twenty dollars for fifteen minutes. Later this same doctor, speaking before a medical board, said that in all his years of practice I was the only patient who, when told she had no T.B., had sworn at him. I hadn't. I had merely said, 'Didn't I tell you so? You make me tired, you doctors and your damned decisions.'

After I was settled, I wrote Mrs. Armstrong that my manuscript had been returned, but that the editor had written a very encouraging letter. Oh, Editors, how we hang on your every word! I shall never forget the upheaval one caused by writing me that a story wasn't 'significant.' It was the first time I had met that word — 'had occasion to use it,' as Sam Weller would say.

'May 30. Seven A.M. I hear the nurses singing before beginning the day's work. It is sweet, but they are better as nurses than as prima donnas. Have received Earl's thanks for gift (a watch chain of gold nuggets belonging to his father), also his Commencement announcement on which he wrote, "I owe it all to you, Mother." I expect he does. Sometimes I wonder if it is a good debt. Would it have been better for him to have found his feet earlier? I don't think so. Anyway, he has not had to take the struggle of life so young. Is it best? Time will tell. How I long to start a family line who are not job-hunters, who are not struggling so hard to live that they may have a chance to live. I wish I could draw by main force from my mind the thoughts, hopes, aspirations I have. These things I do write are so inadequate.

'June 29. Six A.M. Last night I heard them calling an extra. I expect Al Smith is nominated. Since the convention I think more of Mrs. Smith. The wife of a man as bright as Al, who is allowed to go unattended to Houston among the wily politicians and raving reporters and who is trusted not to talk too much, must be some woman.

'July 17. Six A.M. Just been out and looked

at the day. I have four lovely blue — a blue that makes me clasp my hands in joy — morning-glories hanging over my window.'

I find nothing in life so interesting as human beings. At this time in the sanitarium was a particularly interesting group which visited me each day. Olive, who lived outside, came occasionally, always very smart and stylish in spite of crutches, and most entertaining.

There was Mr. Maxfield, an American gentleman, who had been ill a long time and who lived in the Methodist Sanitarium for years. Possibly some of the kindly spirit shown there came from him. He was one of the finest gentlemen I've ever known, and somehow, even when he was at his worst, one never felt that he was ill. He stayed in the Pavilion, a long cottage containing six tiny rooms with a common porch running its full length. In Mr. Maxfield's time there is no telling how many men had lived in the Pavilion, young men mostly, who had come and gone their way, some cured, many on their last journey. To everyone, irrespective of birth, money, nationality, or creed, he was friend, example, and teacher. He taught them first to conquer their fears, to fight, and to dress and be interested in reading and a garden. He also taught them patience, sanitation, manners and morals. All this he taught without letting them know that they were being taught. I think he didn't even know himself that he was teaching them.

He never came to my cottage without a small gift; papers, a book, or flowers raised in a small space between two cottages. In this space he found room for several varieties of flowers, a few stepping-stones, of which two were pieces of pine board, and a bird bath. Once he brought me a fern he had grown from a tiny one purchased at the ten-cent store. He never came that I did not feel better for his coming. Just by his manner and look he influenced me, and the people in this world who have, or can, or do, influence me are few and far between. I wanted to use better English, to be more of a lady, to be less flippant, less showy-off. He was a man who never said 'I,' but always 'you.' He would ask me all about mining camps and people and be so deeply interested that I would outdo myself, and be almost

breathless in my effort to supply the knowledge which he seemed so to crave. I don't
imagine that ever he was heard to say, 'I
wouldn't, I don't think, I don't like, I judge,
or I believe.' Once Bauer, an Austrian who
lived in the Pavilion and who hated an Italian
also living there, unburdened his heart by telling of the Italian's many failings and crimes.
He ended by what he thought the worst crime
of all: 'What do you think? That damned
Dago swore in front of Mr. Maxfield!'

Bauer, clean, well-dressed, swaggering, had
been in the war under hard-boiled Hungarian
officers, fighting in the High Alps against Italians whom he hated. He told me that when
the Armistice came they were in the midst of a
fierce battle and that their hatred of each
other was such that when ordered to throw
down their arms they continued to fight with
their fists. He told me of suffering and cruel-
ties. He himself was cruel. Another picture,
which I liked better, was of him making Christmas gifts for his family. He crouched in the
snow, whittling from the bark of a tree tiny
boxes in which to put finger rings made of
horseshoe nails. In every ring the owner's in-

itials were inlaid with copper. Each week Bauer brought his little girl's letters for me to read, lovely letters, all unusual because Bauer and her mother neither read nor wrote in English. Always each letter ended with 'God bless you in everything you say or do.'

Another visitor was an elderly Jew, talking business and money, chafing at his sickness, haunted with the fear that it was sent on him as a punishment because of the great wrong he had done a woman, whom he had loved and still loved.

There was Alex, a young Armenian, handsome, eager, charming, studious. During the war, when he and his three younger brothers and sisters were children, the Turks invaded their village and killed the men, Alex's father among them, and then burned the homes. Driving the women and children before them, they started a march, going nowhere in particular, just traveling, camping at night along the way beside the road in barns or corrals. Can't you see these women and children all bearing burdens? Even the smallest child must carry his load. They had their entire belongings with them, bedding, food, clothes.

Alex, besides helping to carry his sister, had cooking utensils tied on him clanking at every step. Also he had in his care a manuscript, written by his father, which contained a history of Armenia.

This is how Alex happened to mention the heavy manuscript: At the corner of one of his eyes was a scar which resembled the scars sometimes left on babies who were helped into the world by the aid of instruments. Always I want to know about everything. Curiosity? Not altogether. It's because, I think, I'm interested in every human creature. So I asked Alex about it. He blushed bright red, then haltingly told about the manuscript. For weeks he carried it. One night they were herded into a cattle shed. At one side, built on the ground, a fire burned, and over this some of the women, Alex's mother among them, were preparing food. In assembling supper this anxious mother had Alex bring to her his burden of pans, kettles, etc. She was poking the fire when she glanced sharply at him and asked where the manuscript was. Alex had to admit that on the road that day he had lost it. Then this overwrought (lovely, too — Alex proudly showed me a picture of her beautiful, refined face), tortured mother, without thinking hit him in the head with the poker.

Alex said that some of the grandmothers slumped beside the road and were left there. The younger women were ravished at night by Turkish soldiers. All this he did not tell easily, willingly. His only wish was to forget. No, there was another wish, one above and beyond everything, that burned into his heart. He longed to get well, return to Armenia, and fulfill his vengeance against the Turks.

There was Kim, a Korean student sent to this country to attend one of our large universities. He was very intellectual and a poet. He read me several of his poems, all written in his precise, artistic characters. First he read in Korean, then interpreted in English. One went something like this: 'There are many roses [girls] here which I could have for the picking, but I think only of my own squash blossom.'

He told me that in Korea they have a plum tree of which they are very fond. It grows in the high mountains and is late blooming. For me he made a poster embellishing it in Korean writing, which he said was 'Anne Ellis, plum blossom amid the snow.'

He told me that his people thought much of learning, little of soldiering, and that the oldest culture had come from Korea, then China. The Japanese he considered mere barbarians, who by might had taken Korea, and he said that the Koreans were waiting for the time when Japan would have her hands full with war — with the United States, Kim hoped — then Korea would step to the front and regain her independence.

'But, Kim,' I would say, 'war is unthinkable. People have developed understanding, and there will never be another big war.'

'We are waiting,' Kim replied.

Today, as I write this, Japan is engaged in a terrible invading war — a war that may entangle the world before it is finished. And Korea waits.

CHAPTER XVII

Don't let the song die out of your heart.
ANNIE WADDELL

Nor the dream fade away from your mind.
A. E.

'AUGUST 20, '28. Yesterday I saw Herbert Hoover, who may be the next President of the United States. Anyway, that is what Senator Cutting, looking English and bored, promised when he introduced him very ably. Right now Herbert Hoover is finding it a job to do what is expected of him, and as time goes on he is going to find it a harder one. He's too set a man for a grandstand effect — a stolid speaker, who does not exhilarate, and leaves an audience cold, rather let-down. Mrs. Hoover looks like a President's wife, except when she smiles. Then she looks like me, with her teeth far apart in front. She is a politician and is enjoying herself. I could see her from where I stood, nudging his elbow or pulling at his sleeve in order to make him notice or shake hands with one of the sweating, cold crowd who only cheered when invited

and waved their arms when told to do so. I
expect most of them were T.B.'s and not given
to arm-waving. Governor Dillon, handsome,
disillusioned, and Stafford, beaming every
minute in the picture, were there, too. Both
crowd and politicians were relieved when the
train pulled out.'

This day I saw something that affected me
much more than the Hoovers. Alex was es-
corting me, helping me on and off busses, up
and down steps, when a parading woman
startled me and I grabbed Alex's arm.

'Alex, do you see what I see?' Alex, trained
by Mr. Maxfield, knew that he shouldn't
make personal comments, so he didn't. Again
the woman passed us. I stopped dead in my
tracks and looked at her. Then I said to
Alex, 'Bare legs! Aren't they terrible?'

This was the time when skirts, along with
the stock market, had reached a new high.
Alex thought I was prudish and said so. But
I protested:

'Oh, not that, Alex. I wouldn't care if she
was naked, provided that she was beautiful.
It's because they are ugly. Bare legs in any-

[207]

body over six years are so raw and coarse and bruised-looking, and hairy. Oh, I hope many won't follow this fad!'

'August 21. Today I'm to have a wisdom tooth pulled, and as soon as I'm able must have new glasses. These decaying shells! Never in my life have I been so contented. Is it because I have no irritations and have had a few words of praise for my writing? These I keep in a large envelope marked "My Hope Chest," and read them daily. Just now I have so little regard for money that when my hand itches I don't scratch it on wood.

'August 26. It turned out to be two teeth. I'm sore in mouth and spirit. But a letter and magazines came from S—— wanting me to try and work some of my material into such shape that they could use it. It looks as though sometime I am really going to make it. Thank God, thank God, and I'm glad I've been sick!

'September 1. I waver between Hoover and Smith and "could be happy with either, were t'other dear charmer away." I'm a Republican with Democratic leanings. I suppose the

Democrats are just as bad as the Republicans, but I don't know it.

'September 8. Yesterday a letter from Earl, saying he was considering buying an engagement ring on the installment plan. He said that he wanted to get it in order that Arline could have it for her "engagement party." Time was when I would have considered this poor business, and poor taste. Now I think it the thing to do. Anything not hurtful, though it may be poor business or foolish, is the thing to do, if it makes for happiness.

'September 24. Sick. Adrenaline, disappointment. Between attacks one forgets the horror of asthma as one does labor pains. Even the book has taken a back seat in my mind. The First American celebration starts today, part of what is to us the passing show of life in which we can take no part. Doing no writing except in my dreams. Last night Miss M. hemorrhaged. This A.M. people are hushed and a little afraid, hoping September will soon be over. It seems August and September are hemorrhage months.

'October 1. High fever and pulse, pain in my side. Nurses say I'm sick. I feel no worse than usual except eyes hurting, hands and feet burning. I can't write or even think. Can it be, I wonder, the beginning of the condition "All is over now, the hope, the joy and the sorrow"?

'October 3. Still doing business at the old stand. Neuritis, mustard plasters, pleurisy, pain, hot-water bottles, also pills and capsules taking their turn. Think I will try and write tomorrow. "Struggle" about finished. Have been getting my prize prohibition letter ready. [William Durant $25,000 prize for a workable plan to enforce prohibition. I sent a short, sweet one which would have worked and should have won.] But have been so peeved with prohibitioners that I'm almost driven to drink. People here rant against Smith, saying it's because he is wet, when really it's because of his being Catholic. Warring religions, to an innocent bystander, are confusing, to say the least, and not at all confidence-giving. Too bad something couldn't have happened to Mabel Willebrandt right after the Republican Convention. Then we were proud of her, proud of her knowledge, dignity, and Johnny-on-the-spotness over the credentials committee. There she was doing something constructive, leading one to think that, after all, women might make good in politics, but she must spill the beans by mixing church, politics, and prohibition.

'October 1. I wish hope came in the form of a pill so that when one felt the need of it one would have it at hand. For over a month I've been just drifting, not expecting much. Now since I'm better again, I plan. Just this A.M. I've published three books and numerous short stories, built me a home, helped all my relatives, traveled some, and eaten a lot. All this, even to the clothes, has been definitely settled, while the question before the house is whether to take a bed-bath or risk going to the building for one, and whether it would be wise to take off a raspy oil-soaked blanket jacket the nurses have pinned on me with large safety pins. I'm trying to finish "Struggle." It is work and not coming so easily or so well. Recently a writing friend said to me, "If I'm not in the mood, not feeling top-notch, I cannot write, can you?"

'"I don't know," I answered. "Sometime I'd like to try it and see."'

Here I may say that all my writing is done in bed, the tablet resting on my lap.

'Although, like D. H. Lawrence, I never feel really ill or that I am an invalid. He said: "But the bronchials and asthma are awful — I say, as the ancients say there is an evil world soul, which sometimes overpowers one. I feel so strongly as if my illness weren't really me. I feel perfectly well and all right — *in my self*, yet there is this beastly torturing chest superimposed on me, and it's as if there was a demon lived there, triumphing and extraneous to me. I do feel it extraneous to me. I feel perfectly well, even perfectly healthy, till the devil starts scratching and squeezing and I feel perfectly awful. So what's to be done? Doctors frankly say they don't know."

'October 10. I've been stepping out, first to town trying to buy a hat, having had my last one four years. If I were saying this in front of a husband, I'd moan. It is work for me to buy a hat. I have an extra large head, and long hair which all salespeople insist I must wear differently so that every hat they try on will fit. I wanted either a blue or

purple, came home with a black — six-fifty.
Then a charming girl came selling tickets to
Democratic banquet at Franciscan. I bought
one and went, enjoying every minute. At
every plate were little chocolate donkeys carrying a silk flag. A good meal, music and
speeches. But what pleased me most were
Negro waiters, both men and women, well
poised and dressed in plain white. Such a
rest from the rouged, earringed, pearl-beaded,
gaudily dressed whites! A very enthusiastic
crowd declaring Al will be elected. I'm betting
on him and rather hoping he will be, but my
reason and political sense say he won't.

'October 30. A decided wheeze — too much
party. Last night Mr. Maxfield came to
visit and found me plastered and just dripping
cold cream. Emily Price Post has neglected
to say what to do in a case of this kind, so I
laughed and wiped it off. Alex is showing
color [hemorrhaging]. Too bad. I've sent
him an Al Smith donkey. Yesterday I finished "Struggle."

'November 5, '28. The other evening a
woman speaker said the only farm relief that
New Mexico needed was rain. Today we are

getting it. Nurses carrying the iodine and swabs right with them. (Patients in cold weather are painted for pleurisy.) Tomorrow we elect a new President. If this campaign had gone on much longer and if we believed all we heard, no man on either side would be fit to elect.

'November 14. I've been sick. Last night heard over neighbor's radio Al Smith give farewell, almost promise speech. There's a man for you. He may be President yet. [Today, May 2, '32, he is trying for nomination.] Several of us went up to university to hear Sousa's Band. When we came out there was a wonderful sunset. I stopped in the rain and enjoyed it.

'November 21. One year ago I left Albuquerque for Phoenix. A letter from Arline telling me all about her announcement. I must write Earl how to act at a church wedding, although I've never seen one. How I want to see this one! At nights I plan how, if the Durant Prohibition plan should win, I would charter an airship and at the last minute fly to Salida and be one among that wedding party. Last night I went to see

"Abie's Irish Rose." I liked it. Anne Nichols appeared in person and a wonderful fur coat. She is staying at Jamez, with a sick relative. On Tuesday I went down and met, or rather waited for, Lucy Fitch Perkins's train, which was four hours late. Mrs. Perkins looks just as I thought she would, a lovely lady. Wonder what she thought of me. I was tired, and cold, and had a wisp of hair hanging down. Is there anything in a name? The greatest hero on Vestres named Lionel Licoric.

'November 29. Today got "Such is Life" off to S——, hope they like it. Never a Thanksgiving in my life I have not been thankful, never so much as today. The first holiday I haven't rebelled at not being with my family.

'December 5. Yesterday I was sunk and in a fair way to have the blues. Today for some reason I feel better. I know it will come out all right. A letter from Earl telling me of wedding arrangements. And he in debt head over heels! Hunted out the white embroidered centerpiece Olive made for me to send them for a wedding gift, then decided I wanted to keep it myself. Have been writing a reminiscence for the "Tribune," supposed to be one thousand words. I wrote what I thought was enough, counted them and had twenty-five hundred. I wish words were not so easy.

'December 1. Am still waiting for mail. Patiently? Well, more patiently. From being tragic it's getting to be funny. Evening — and not so funny. My sketches returned from S——. It's queer how, when my writing is praised and I read the manuscript, it sounds good. Then if it is turned down and I re-read the same manuscript it sounds so terrible I almost blush for it. Can I stand it if all these new hopes crumble? I can and will, but life would be mighty dreary. Maybe it's all been a mirage — a pleasant one. Maybe I can't write, I don't know. If I did I would say "I will put it over," and I would, but I wouldn't want to fight for any worthless thing. When I have these back-setting times, life seems too long. Then when hope returns it seems too short. I suppose instead of losing faith in my authorship I should write a "Lady's Feelings on the Return of a Manuscript." Just now I'm swallowing hard and singing, "Lady, make your mind up to wait your life away." When, in thought, I'm riding the high tide of hope, I see myself making enough to live on in a modest house in some warm place, feeling in a small way worth while and to a certain extent successful. Then on the other side I'm almost afraid to think. There would be the letting Mrs. A. off from this charity. I see myself somewhere, Earl and Neita keeping me, getting on very cheaply. I can do this. I'm trained, praying for death cheerfully, because I'm darned if I'll let Fate get my goat. My head may be bloody, also bowed, but thank whatever is, my guts are still on the job.

'December 23. The robin has returned. I say this because once Nellie Burget Miller said to me, "If one threw a stone at a robin it would stop singing." She meant disappointments to writers, when they think they can't and won't write again. While my spirit is not soaring as it would have had I had good news of the book, it is still happy and hopeful. I am feeling better than I have felt for two years, and expect a Merry Christmas and Prosperous New Year.

'Evening — A letter from Mrs. Perkins

saying that she is sending me one of her books. I'm glad.

'December 24, 1928. Well, Anne, we salute you. Today was a red-letter day. The wire from Houghton Mifflin Company accepting my book made it so. At once I wired Neita, Earl, and Mrs. Armstrong that they might be happy with me. The one thing that I wished hardest for seems possible — that I might make my living and be independent. Thank, oh, thank, whatever is!

'December 27. And I did not win Durant's twenty-five thousand dollars. Well, anyway, many nights I entertained myself spending it. Another year about gone. Taking it all in all, a good year. Here's to you, 1929.'

CHAPTER XVIII

Life repeats itself and always yields its sweet to those who bravely drink its bitter.

IDA M. TARBELL

'JANUARY 15. This A.M. finds me going on a milk diet. I really feel too bad to enjoy my good luck, but if it weren't for this luck life would be unbearable.

'January 17. Sick, so much that I fear — no, I will never fear death, only now it would be less welcome.'

The reason for milk diet was that the publishers, I knew, would want a picture for the book. I was dreadfully thin and had no thought of appearing in a book that way. I understood that one could gain weight on milk, so, in spite of not liking it, and realizing that it is bad for asthma, on a milk diet I went.

During this trying time the book came to have my final 'once over.' Two chapters had been left without headings and, as I was too ill to think, I reached out blindly and picked up one of Robert Service's books, where I found one heading. The other I dragged from my poor befuddled brain. Character sketches had been left out. The editor said she didn't see that they added to the book, but in my opinion they were the book. I was determined they were going in, so sick as I was I just poked them in anywhere, much the same as one would poke plums into a cake.

A clause in my contract stated that any other books written by me must first be submitted to my publishers. This, of course, prevented me from sending 'Struggle' to the 'Atlantic.' Later it was finished and published under the title of 'Plain Anne Ellis.'

'March 26. Sick. So very sick that it seems unbearable. After dying with the utmost agony yesterday, today I am free again. Sometime during this hell I wrote to an asthma doctor in Boston. Today his answer came. He says that he is no wizard and that he does not cure all asthmatics. Still, sometime I'm going to see him.'

Queer about that letter. One day a man who

once had asthma came to call on me. There's a close bond between asthmatics. He was the only person I've met who has experienced suffering greater than mine. He had spent a fortune and finally was cured by a Boston specialist, who took only a few patients and whose fee ran into thousands of dollars.

One night in my distress, numb with suffering and half doped, I decided to visit this doctor and planned to hitch-hike on my hands and knees to Boston and sit on his doorstep and choke and cough until he took me in. The next morning, while still not quite right in my mind, I wrote him a letter. I don't know what I said — I wish I did — only this, which makes me smile: 'I have no money, but if you will have me for a patient, and I live, sometime I will pay you.' He, a great specialist, answered that crazy letter and sent vaccine. He also said there was no need for me to come to Boston, and for me to send him a specimen when the weather grew colder, and he would make vaccine. But I was going to Boston, and I wrote my banker friend in Saguache to sell my house for whatever it would bring.

'March 28. A little better, but still a miserable object. Sunday is Easter. How wonderful to have new clothes and be able to wear them! I have had no new clothes in years, have not been dressed since Christmas, and have had no bath since September, except for a nurse whipping a wet rag around over me. But today I have ordered a tin washtub and will have a real bath to celebrate Easter. Also the fun of breaking a foolish rule.

'March 30. So sick — I want to cry, "I just can't stand it." But what good would it do? There is no space between what we can stand and death. Neither comes nor goes at our will. And to cap the stack, I'm too weak to have bath and the tub is hidden in the closet.

'April 22. Not able to have that bath until 17th. My home, that I was years in building, and my furniture, have sold for $775. Jose packed up some of my things. Judging from her letter, it made her very sad. Mrs. Gann has taken the limelight from the Hoovers and I do wish, after she's fairly seated, Curtis would up and get married.

'May 8. Today I am going to town and sit

or slump for a picture. Proofs of the book here.
The type is good, make-up fine, and writing
readable. It is thrilling to see one's words in
print.'

The next entry in the diary, scrawled across
two pages and almost unreadable, is my last
will and testament.

Since the book was to be published in
August, all photographs had to be in the
publisher's hands by the first of June. By
this time I was drinking five quarts of milk
each day and had gained weight.

I had the nurse lay out my dress — a blue
georgette which had seen long service, first
for one of my friends and later for me. With
it I wore a lace collar and cuffs that I had
made from scraps of lace; also my cape, worn
for so many years that even the birds knew it.
For a wonder my hair went up at the first
try — a good thing, too, since my hands were
so weak.

The nurse called a taxi and helped me into
it. Only after being indoors so long do we fully
realize what a beautiful place the world is.

When I arrived I found that I must climb

a flight of steps. This about finished me. Then I thought, 'Now's a hot time for you to give up, after consuming all that milk, too. Now go on. Remember you have to go only a step at a time, so up with you.'

I made it and fell into a chair. The artist — yes, he was an artist — brought me a drink. After I had rested he told me to put on lipstick, but no powder. Lipstick? I sat trembling and sweating. I had never used it, and didn't know how. When the artist returned, I told him so, and he instructed me patiently how to get it out of the tube.

'Use enough,' he said, 'merely to outline the lips.'

Then he tried to pose me. He unclasped my clenched hands and placed them, palms upward, placidly in my lap; but before he could turn around they were clenched again. After taking me in several postures, he gave up. We both knew it was a poor job, but my strength was gone, and my only wish was to fall into bed. I returned to the little room, threw my cape around me, pulled my hat down, bringing part of my hair with it, and staggered blindly through the door.

Then the artist said:

'Let's try another, just as you are. Sit there — never mind your hands. Now throw up your head, your shoulders. Fine — a little more life. You can do it — good!'

The resulting photograph is used in 'Life of an Ordinary Woman.' He surely was an artist.

After this I was sick. The nurses made me have a doctor. When he came he asked what was the trouble, and I said, 'Nothing, now that I haven't asthma.'

He laughed.

A real doctor — the first one to look below the belt line, where it seemed a gall bladder was cutting up and needed cutting out. I went, therefore, to the Presbyterian Sanitarium for an operation. Always I had felt the lack of an operation — socially, I mean. By now I knew that I was desperately ill, and didn't care. My only regret was in not living to see the reviews of my book.

I sent word to none of my people and left the strictest instructions that no word was to be sent except in case of death. The doctor made all the arrangements, two special nurses were employed, and the torture was on. I remember only their trying to get me to swallow fruit juices thick with sugar, also a devilish invention called a Murphy drip, and a vine outside the window where linnets came, linnets that chirruped, lived their time and died. I wished that I was a linnet. I asked if a gall-bladder operation was about the same as having an appendix out.

When the nurse said, 'About five times more difficult,' I felt really important.

Now, quietly, to myself I had made all arrangements. I was prepared for the future, be it oblivion or life, and wrote in my diary —

'June 1–2 (it was the 3rd). "Just before the battle, mother," and I'm thinking of everything and nothing. Earl is to have ten dollar gold piece and shawl. Mrs. Armstrong is to be paid, if ever anything is left to pay with. Everything else is to be equally divided between Neita and Earl. All my love. A. E.'

Before I went on the table a nurse took my history. She asked questions about finances, which was to be expected; about religion, which was all right; about my family history, which I answered, although I could not see that it mattered whether they died with their boots on or on an operating table; but when she asked my grandmother's maiden name, it was too much, and, angelic as I felt, I laughed and said, 'Search me.'

CHAPTER XIX

Character is measured not by a person's reaction to success; but by his reaction to the success of others.

NEITA CAREY

I WAS ready and waiting, annoyed that the doctors were slow in coming. The doctor gave me a hypodermic, a super-de-luxe hypodermic. Like smooth oil it ran through my tortured body, warming, soothing, as it went. My doctor had been physician for seven years at the Court of Siam. Ordinarily I say 'doctor,' as it is easier to spell, but somehow 'doctor' seems inappropriate when connected with courts.

The rest is memory flashes. Whiteness — oval white light, many white forms, running water. 'You should write it for the medical journal.' They say I didn't hear this, but I did. Alcohol applied lightly in long, soothing strokes. The crying of newborn babies. Footsteps coming and going.

Then, outside my closed door, whisperings — 'She cannot have visitors.'

Then, 'Well, she's going to have me.' And Jose, followed by Ben, walked in.

'Oh, Jose,' I said, 'I told them not to send for you unless I died.'

She said, 'What would be the use in coming if you were dead?'

Jose always hits the nail on the head.

The next morning Earl and Arline walked in. They had ridden all night, just as Ben and Jose had, Arline, fearing they might be held up, in the dark on a lonely road, had hidden her rings. Where do you suppose? On the inside of her ears, and then pulled her hair down over them.

That afternoon, believe it or not, in came Neita from Phoenix. Of course I couldn't talk or move, and when I was moved fell into a huddle of skin and bones, but I could listen. How they visited! I had forgotten the keen wit and tongue of Jose. She told all the Saguache County news, especially that of Bonanza where we had lived as children, and where she always had lived. Ellis, her daughter, had just graduated from Saguache High School, from which Earl and Neita had also graduated, and all three Commencements were revived — the clothes, gifts, calamities, honors, hopes, everything. I had forgotten the quiet efficiency of Ben, who never talked much, but who was a master listener and laugher. He is one of those men who see things and fix them without any fuss or feathers. When a window shade went 'fluey,' instead of calling a nurse he quietly took it apart with his pocket knife, mended and rehung it: and when I slipped down in bed, much as the 'Brimstone Barker' did in 'Bleak House,' instead of throwing a pillow, as her husband did, Ben gently lifted or turned me. Earl and Arline gave me all the details of their wedding, what was 'et and said and done.' They told me about their work, prospects and plans, things that somehow never get into letters. Neita told humorously, as only she can tell, the ups and downs of the Carey family, and how just now she had broken quarantine with Jack in bed, and a smallpox sign on the house. For years we hadn't relaxed from life's battle long enough to gossip, feeling that we couldn't afford it. Still now that I was dying we could afford it, and we made the most of it.

So I listened and laughed inside, but showed no signs of being anything except alive. Then my nurse tried to open the closet door, which had been sticking. She pulled and yanked. I was annoyed and called Neita, with my eyes. When she bent over me, I whispered, 'In God's name, why doesn't somebody smear soap on that door where it catches?'

Neita threw up her head, beamed proudly at the others, and said, 'The old bean still works.' It was the most slangy phrase I ever heard her use.

A good time was had by all. When tired I had only to close my eyes to drift away somewhere. On one of these journeys I had a vision. I was in a world of moving octagon disks. I was a disk. We all had stamped on us designs something like Chinese characters. The designs varied in beauty. As each disk moved and lived, it helped to create the design on every disk with which it came in contact, and in turn its own design was influenced by these contacts. When finished they were fitted into a marvelous opalescent, mother-of-pearl screen which was enveloped in living light. I saw, when my design was completed, the very place I was to fill. None of us knew what our symbols stood for, and while each saw the designs being shaped on every other, no one could see his own, except dimly, when they shifted or eddied into the screens radiating light. Once when I came quite close I saw my symbols. They were angular, misshapen. I worried. I wanted to be beautiful; to add beauty to beauty. Again I drifted away and was glad — glad to be given time to reshape those emblems before coming into the presence of the only one who understood the meaning, could read the writing, the Master-Builder.

The special nurses were with me five or six days, and I discovered what real nursing was. When the night nurse, a tiny little thing, wasn't doing something for me, which she was if I made the slightest movement, she sat bolt upright in a chair beside the bed and slept. I've awakened and seen her there with flushed face, hair all rumpled, like a tired baby gone to sleep in its high chair.

When these nurses left, a hospital nurse dressed the place on my side which my doctors gloated over and called a beautiful piece of work, but which to me resembled a huge torpid centipede gone red.

When I was able, an ambulance moved me back to the Methodist Sanitarium, where Neita stayed with me a month. After all my bills were paid, there was left from my house money thirty dollars. On this I decided to have a fling. Don't smile — wait till you hear. Both Neita and I were born with a love of beauty, which is more often tortured than pleased by man-made things. La Fonda, in Santa Fé, was to me utterly eye and soul satisfying, and I intended to treat Neita and myself to one night there, trusting nobody would ever hear of our extravagance. We went and engaged one of the best rooms. We were invited for dinner to the house of a friend, where cocktails were served. In spite of the fact that I had lived almost my entire life in supposedly rough Western mining camps, where there were saloons on every corner, and whiskey, in case of emergency, in every home, this was my first sight, taste, or smell of cocktails. I swallowed mine with — no, not gusto, almost aversion — but I swallowed it. So this was the concoction without which no entertainment was complete, no story could be written, no play played, which was upsetting a country economically, politically, and religiously. Gosh!

At dinner we had wine and I waxed warmer and grew more talkative — which is some talkative. Neita looked distressedly at me. I thought that she thought that so soon after an operation I was overdoing. As I hate being dictated to, I pretended that I thought she was censuring my wildly gesturing hands, and, to put her in her place, I said, 'Neita thinks I am pointing, which reminds me of a story about a woman, rough and ready, who in various ways had made a stake in Alaska's boom days. She returned to San Francisco, bought a lot of fine clothes and hired a woman to train her in the graces of society. She gave a dinner party and everything was going fine when all at once she jumped to her feet, pointed a rigid finger at a man dining at another table, and raged, "There's So and So. I knew him in Nome. The G—d—s—of-a-b—" Then her arm dropped, she wilted, and turned to her social mentor, pleading, "Oh, pardon me for pointing." I, of course, dashed it just as it's written. I'm Victorian, and a "damn" is as strong as I go.'

[234]

Somehow Neita looked more distressed than ever and hastened our departure, but when we arrived in La Fonda, I found that her trouble was not fear lest I would overdo, or say something wrong, but cocktails. And — was she sick? When things finally subsided, Neita's stomach among them, we got into bed — such luxurious, soft beds — too soft. We weren't used to this kind and threatened to remove the covers and take to the floor. We tossed, turned, and finally dozed, when I was struck with the thought that I hadn't seen the typewriter. I wakened Neita.

'Where is the typewriter?'

We got up and looked. It was lost. Some fling! And so to bed.

The next day Neita left for Phoenix, and I, with the discovered typewriter, for Bonanza, where I was to spend the summer with Jose. How I loved it! I felt reborn and reveled in life. The book came out August 23. By way of celebration Jose used her marvelous embroidered table-cover and some of her famous ruffled petunias.

When almost two weeks had passed without a word from any person who had read the book, I thought, 'If I've written a book that neither peeves nor pleases, I'm a failure.' Then the letters began to pile in and haven't stopped to this day — interesting, appreciative, astounding, wonderful letters. And the reviews! Oh, my friends, those reviews were worth living for! But here's a queer thing — the letters and reviews praised me more than the book, which honestly surprised me.

And how did my home town take it? Well — but why bring that up? Let's talk about roses. I will share one of my letters with you:

'MY DEAR ANNE ELLIS: — Some good Christian sent me a copy of your book, and all the affairs of my life, including eating and sleeping, have been demoralized until just now, when I have come to the end.

'But I want to tell you, you simply must not stop in the middle of the story like this. I want to know what happened then! When one has lived with another person, as I have lived with you through these three hundred pages, I simply cannot leave you like this! I must know how you get along.

'Your book is a throbbing human story,

[236]

revealing the heart and mind of a woman who might be called "Everywoman." You may not know much about the technique of writing (I mean you have not studied it), but you surely have the gift of revelation. You have opened a window in your own soul, and those of us who have been privileged to look through it, have lived and laughed and suffered with you.

'But I want to know that you have found rest and peace for your soul. I want you to have music and pictures, and all the books in the world, and a chance to see London and the Bay of Naples. I want you to have your breakfast in bed, and a membership in a reading club, and the Book-of-the-Month Club, a manicure every Saturday, and a box at the theater, and everything else you have ever wanted. Sincerely yours.'

When I answered, I told her that I not only had breakfast in bed, but dinner and supper as well; that I had never in my life had a manicure nor been in a beauty shop. And, because she wrote such a good letter, I complacently suggested she try to write, assuring her that I didn't find it hard at all and that I believed she could do it.

Months afterward I discovered — not from her — that she was one of Canada's most noted authors with many books to her credit!

'The Life of an Ordinary Woman' was included among the forty notable American books of 1929 selected by the American Library Association for the League of Nations. The list prepared for the International Institute of Intellectual Co-operation of the League of Nations says, 'The works should be selected from those dealing with an important subject or from the pen of an original and interesting author.'

In October I went up to Denver, expecting to spend the winter with Earl and Arline. But at this late day I even hate to write it — my asthma started and daily grew worse. My only hope was to send to Boston for vaccine. I should have despaired but for the thought of that vaccine. We watched for the mailman, and Earl rushed out the day it came and returned haltingly. The bottle was broken!

Here I was in Denver, helpless, and that high-priced, temperamental specialist — or so we understood — in Boston. It was almost impossible to reach him at any price, but he was my only hope, and Earl wired him. Again the mail-carrier left a small package. Again Earl ran to get it. Again Earl unwrapped the container and — it was broken! Let us draw a curtain over that helpless, hopeless, huddled piece of humanity, moaning like a hurt animal, which was me.

Doctor W—— not only a great specialist, but a great man as well — again sent vaccine, which arrived intact and helped me immediately.

CHAPTER XX

Not enjoyment and not sorrow,
Is our destined end or way.
But to work that each tomorrow
Finds us farther than today.
                    HENRY W. LONGFELLOW

As I found that Denver was too cold, I moved on to New Mexico and the Methodist Sanitarium, where I improved steadily. I wanted to be with the Careys in Arizona for Christmas. Shortly after I arrived there, I became ill; heart, asthma, doctors, nurses, etc. Plenty of etc.!

When recovering from this attack, I really did a brave deed. Twice in my life I've been brave. Other times, when doing something seemingly so, I did it because it was the only thing to do. And perhaps, because it was done under compulsion, we should not count one of these times, which was holding, by the means of fire-tongs clamped on his tail, a rampant skunk while my mother stood off with a rifle and shot him. So that brings us to the one time I showed real bravery, or maybe it was just foolishness. They are so closely related, it's often hard to judge between the two.

The Phoenix Biltmore Hotel at stated times sponsored an afternoon devoted to books and the reviews of books. On one of these occasions, I was invited to speak. Now, in my life I had attended no clubs, never heard a book reviewed, and never since the age of eight spoken before an audience. The latter, however, I kept secret. Neita supposed that in my political campaigns I had made many speeches.

I wanted and prayed for strength to go. I wanted to hear how my book, any book, was reviewed. Then — and this is the main reason — I am always keenly interested to know how the woman which is me will act under all conditions and circumstances. I never do know. She often surprises me and very often peeves me. I seldom praise her, but do have the best time laughing at her antics. There's one thing I can always depend on her doing, however much she promises not to. She will talk too much, often out of turn, always without thinking. Invariably, when I get home, I say, 'You fool,' or in extreme cases, 'You damned fool,' and in very extreme cases, 'You damned old fool.'

So, day by day, I prayed and planned. Neita often asked, 'Don't you think I'd better tell them you will not be able to go?' And each time, I, determined to go, would beg her to wait a few days longer. Then,

'Mama, in case you do go, have you thought of what you are going to talk about?'

'Oh, yes,' I told her, 'it's all prepared.' I lied. Every atom of my strength was concentrated on merely being able to go.

The day came and I, who had not been out of bed in weeks, sat up in a chair and dressed, not in my best, but in a friendly dress that had 'set me' for over ten years — a soft black wool embroidered in white and made at night when Earl and I were sitting around the stove, he studying, I resting from the office work. The first time I had worn it with a corsage of red geraniums, a girl home from college had said I looked 'doggy.' I didn't know whether it was a compliment or a slam.

I was helped to a car and rode to the Biltmore where crowds of women were pouring in. I did not look around, but closed my eyes and clenched my hands to keep from fainting. Once I did look up to see Neita, drawn and anxiously tense, and inside I grinned, thinking, 'Old girl, you would look a darned sight worse if you knew what I do.'

Finally I was introduced and almost blindly, not knowing what I was going to say, I walked to the speaker's table, took a firm hold on myself and talked to those women. I don't know what about. I only saw a huge body with a single head, which, at first, was not eager, or smiling or particularly interested, but seemed tired, a little skeptical, and a good deal bored. But not when I finished, which was soon.

I then had the pleasure — and it was a pleasure — of meeting them. One woman I remember said gushingly, 'You look like a writer,' and my unruly tongue flippantly answered, 'Oh, it's asthma makes me look that way.'

They left, all except one attractive, beautifully dressed woman who came to where I was sitting and introduced herself as Mrs. Marshall. She very kindly said she had read the 'Life of an Ordinary Woman' and had heard the woman talk and enjoyed both, only she used warmer, more gracious words — words that, coming from the widow of Vice-President Marshall, were truly something to be proud of and for that day's doings a reward for valor.

As spring advanced and days grew warmer and cottonwood trees filled the air with snow, my hay fever and asthma also advanced. Once again Fate said to me, 'Move on,' and I didn't know where to go. I didn't want to return to a sanitarium. I was neither physically nor financially able to keep house, that is, without someone interested and living near me who could look in occasionally to see how I was coming on.

One day, when my mind was beset with this lifelong worry, where to go? What to do? I had several callers. We all, as women do, talked at once, telling where we had been, what we had seen, done, and thought; that is, all except one. She had come quietly in and taken the worst seat in the house, where she sat pleasantly silent. I hadn't caught her name — I never do. At one glance I take in a person's clothes from foot to head and never hear their names, and if I should meet them the next day

— unless they wore the same clothes — I should not recognize them.

This woman was dressed in plain sport clothes, and was absolutely unadorned as to jewelry or make-up. Particularly, I noticed her well-shaped legs, ankles, and feet, and that she had the wide-open, wondering, clear-blue eyes of a girl. It was plain to be seen that the other women were interested to see how I looked, dressed, and talked, but she showed only thrill and pleasure, which made me think, 'Poor thing, she can't have been around much or met many people. Why, she's acting just as I would if I should meet a writer.' To myself, I'm not a writer and to myself — never will be a successful one.

I judged, because my visitor said 'idear,' that she was from New England. Because she was so placid and had such an untroubled face, I judged that she was slow, unbusiness-like, and probably lazy. The following shows what a good deducer I am. She was born in Fairfax County, Virginia. Her father owned famous Gunston Hall, where she grew up. She was educated in Washington, at Gunston Hall School, named for her own home. When seventeen she was in London, living with Julia Marlowe and playing a part in her company. Twice she had toured Europe with Miss Marlowe, once with the company and once for pleasure. And there was, is, and always will be between her and Julia Marlowe Sothern a very beautiful friendship. Later she had been several years with the Ben Greet Company, where she met and played with Sybil Thorndyke and where they too started a lifelong friendship.

She had lived the busiest, fullest life and had accomplished many things, such as making a husband and children happy and having two books published, as well as numerous magazine articles. A third book was ready for the publisher. She did all her own housework and was one of the best managers and business women I've ever known.

This day, without seeming to do so, she stepped into the picture and started to manage for me, with the result that in a month's time I was headed for California.

My friend met me at the station and took me directly to my home, two tiny rooms under a big oak tree. This house she had completely furnished with her own things. Waiting on the table was a welcoming meal, kept hot by her lovely daughter, and on the food, the flowers, the rugs, bed, curtains, pictures, books, dishes, everything were pinned pieces of paper on which were printed quotations from 'The Life of an Ordinary Woman.' My friend had even planted a tiny garden which also fluttered with quotations.

But in spite of my lovely surroundings, in a few weeks I was quite ill and was making a new collection of doctors, nurses, medicine, and etc. — still bearing down hard on the etc.! I gave up to die and wrote in my diary:

'August 7, '31. Today I've made up my mind not to get well; also to get me some new clothes and ditch the ones I've had for eleven years. [I didn't.] I've also given up many things in life — a trip to New York, an evening with literary people, seeing a speakeasy, night club, butler, gigolo [I was showing off even in my diary], having a beauty treatment, a large easy-chair, hearing real music, beautiful surroundings, climbing a mountain, pine trees, quaking aspen, Colorado, Santa Fé; also being able to get all my material in shape. How-

ever, I'm going to try and finish "Sunshine Preferred." So, Asthma, I defy you — come on and
do your worst. I shall buy me a rubber ring to
sit in so it doesn't matter how thin I get. I'm going to live in bed, so it doesn't matter how weak
I get. I'll sleep when I can, and when I can't
I'll lie awake and do some plain and fancy
coughing. No more am I going to try to keep
my back straight nor wrinkles out of my brow.
So there, and there, and there! And, damn
you, I may even eat an egg, an onion, or pan-
cakes and sausage, and right now I've a notion
to go and stand in a draught.'

This outburst preceded a sick spell which
subdued rebellion and left me clearer-headed,
sweeter-minded, and determined to fight to the
finish. So that the diary reports:

'I've decided to live, and to have a good time
while doing it. To work when I can. To try to
"stand tall, sit tall, and think tall." I've been
wishing I could do something about the world
depression. I can't, but I can try to lift my
own personal depression, and I will.'

Since food is the most important factor in
any war, I fought my fight along these lines,
fighting unaided by any doctor and without

knowing anything about calories, vitamins, or other what-nots.

In one month I had worked out a diet that helped. At last, after all those years, I'd struck it — so simple, too. For all I know, this diet is against every law of science or medicine, but anyway I'm improving on it and gaining weight.

Each day I'm more convinced that Asthma, the villain of this piece, is a blessing in disguise. It has brought me so much. And I would add to the poet's 'Love the leveler, Time the healer,' 'Illness the fundamental finder,' because it surely teaches one what the fundamentals of happiness really are: Sleep, Food, Peace.

In conclusion, I shall say that I'm living in 'sun-kissed, ocean-washed, island-girded, mountain-guarded Santa Barbara.' Jose is here taking care of me. My family are all well and doing well. My health is better than it has been for years. I am making a living doing interesting work that I love. Who would ask for more? Not I.

THE END